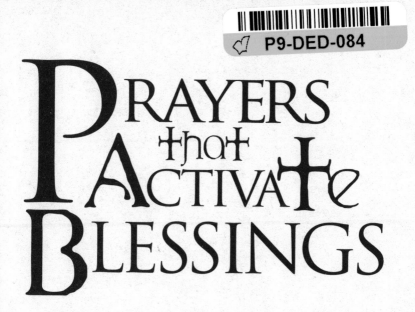

PRAYERS that ACTIVATE BLESSINGS

Prayers that Activate Blessings

John Eckhardt

CHARISMA
HOUSE

Most CHARISMA HOUSE BOOK GROUP products are available at special quantity discounts for bulk purchase for sales promotions, premiums, fund-raising, and educational needs. For details, write Charisma House Book Group, 600 Rinehart Road, Lake Mary, Florida 32746, or telephone (407) 333-0600.

PRAYERS THAT ACTIVATE BLESSINGS by John Eckhardt
Published by Charisma House
Charisma Media/Charisma House Book Group
600 Rinehart Road
Lake Mary, Florida 32746
www.charismahouse.com

Visit the author's website at www.johneckhardt.global.

Library of Congress Cataloging-in-Publication Data:
Eckhardt, John, 1957-
  Prayers that activate blessings / John Eckhardt.
    p. cm.
  ISBN 978-1-61638-370-1 (trade paper) -- ISBN 978-1-61638-427-2 (e-book) 1. Prayer--Christianity. 2. Blessing and cursing. 3. Prayers. I. Title.
  BV227.E35 2011
  248.3'2--dc22

                                    2011011417

20 21 22 23 24 — 18 17 16 15 14
Printed in the United States of America

Contents

Introduction

A Better Understanding of Blessing and Prosperity

T<small>HE SUBJECT OF</small> blessing and prosperity has become very controversial among those in the church. We want to be blessed and live the abundant life Christ died to give us, yet we don't want to approach God as if He is a lottery or a slot machine—if you put in the right amount of prayer, praise, worship, faith, and good works, out comes your blessing. But for some, that is all they see God as, and they get beside themselves when He doesn't come through for them the way they wanted Him to.

Blessing and prosperity are more than money. According to *Strong's Complete Concordance of the Bible*, one Hebrew word for prosperity is *shalom*.

We often associate the word *shalom* with *peace*, but the peace that Christ went to war for on the cross is a complete, whole kind of peace. Also according to Strong's, *shalom* is "completeness, soundness, welfare, and peace." It represents completeness in number and safety and soundness in your physical body. *Shalom* also covers relationships with God and with people.

God's thoughts concerning your peace and prosperity are much higher than you could imagine. It is His desire to bless and prosper you, to give you His grace, favor, and protection. *Favor* means "grace"; "that which affords joy, pleasure, delight, sweetness, charm, loveliness"; and "good will, benefit, bounty, reward." If you look up the Hebrew and Greek definitions of *prosperity*, many of these words carry over into favor as well.

Favor is goodwill. This is God's kindness and benevolence given to those who love Him. Favor will release great blessings, including prosperity, health, opportunity, and advancement. The Bible records numerous examples of God's favor upon His people causing them to experience many breakthroughs. Favor is God's loving-kindness.

Joseph experienced God's favor and went from prison to palace. God will do the same for you. He can change your circumstances in one day no matter where you are in life. This is when the favor of God is on your life.

Job was another man who was blessed and who operated under the full favor and blessing of God. In Job 10:12 he confessed that his life and the favor he had were gifts from God: "Thou hast granted me life and favour, and thy visitation hath preserved my spirit" (KJV). Life and favor are gifts of God. We don't need luck. We need blessing. We need favor. We need the blessing of God. God desires to release new favor on your life. When you have God's favor and blessing, there is nothing in life that can hold you down.

When you begin to walk in the favor and blessing of the Lord, others will recognize it. The favor and blessing of God on your life is one of the most powerful things that can be released to you.

Matthew 6:33 says, "Seek ye first the kingdom of God, and his righteousness; and *all* these things shall be added unto you" (KJV, emphasis added).

Protection was also added to Job. Job 29:17 says, "I brake the jaws of the wicked, and plucked the spoil out of his teeth" (KJV). When the evil plans of the enemy set out to destroy Job, he had weapons to fight back; then he claimed the exponential spoils of the victory.

God says, "You don't need money. You need My favor." You need His shalom—the full measure of peace—to operate in your life. This is your gift from Him if you are His child, if you are in covenant with Him. God blesses His people and rescues them. Just as He did with the Israelites, God loved you and chose you in spite of who you are and what you have done. You are elected by God. You were chosen before the foundation of the world. He chose you. It wasn't because of anything you've done. That is His favor!

God talks to the children of Israel in Ezekiel 16:1–14 about how He found them in a rejected state where they had been thrown away and no one wanted them. They were drowning in their own blood. But when God passed by them, He said to them, "LIVE!" Then He blessed them and adorned them with jewels. God is saying this same thing to you. Maybe you were thrown away to die and had no chance at living. Maybe no one wanted you or you were not born with a silver spoon in your mouth. But when God looked upon you, He had mercy on you.

God will not only save you and wash you, but He will also bless you, dress you up, put jewels on you, and beautify you. The grace and favor of God on your life will cause you to go into a place of prosperity. God not only will save you but will also multiply you and bless you.

In this book we are going to talk about how to obtain the covenant blessing of God. We are going to learn confessions and prayers based on God's Word that will activate His shalom over your life. Death and life are in the power of the tongue. We can choose blessing by choosing to live and speak correctly.

God is ready to release new favor, blessing, prosperity, protection, and peace over you. It is His desire to give you good things. Now get ready to receive them.

BLESSING AND FAVOR DECLARATIONS

Lord, You have granted me life and favor.

Lord, I thank You for life and life more abundantly.

I thank You for favor coming upon my life.

I believe that new life and new favor
have been ordained for me.

Today I receive new life and new favor.

I believe favor is a gift of heaven.

I receive the gift of life—the gift of eternal life.

I receive the gift of favor and the gift of grace
upon my life in the name of Jesus.

Thank You, Lord, for new grace and new favor, new prosperity and new blessing coming on my life.

I am the apple of God's eye.

I am one of God's favorites.

God favors me, loves me, and has chosen me from the foundation of the world to receive His grace and favor.

I receive extraordinary favor on my life in the name of Jesus!

Prayers for the Blessing and Favor of God

Let me be well favored (Gen. 39:6).

Lord, show me mercy and give me favor (Gen. 39:21).

Give me favor in the sight of the world (Exod. 12:36).

Let me be satisfied with your favor like Naphtali (Deut. 33:23).

Let me have favor with You, Lord, and with men (1 Sam. 2:26).

Let me have favor with the king (1 Sam. 16:22).

Let me have great favor in the sight of the king (1 Kings 11:19).

Let me find favor like Esther (Esther 2:17).

Thou hast granted me life and favour, and Thy visitation hath preserved my spirit (Job 10:12, KJV).

I pray unto You, Lord, grant me favor (Job 33:26).

Bless me and surround me with
favor like a shield (Ps. 5:12).

In Your favor is life (Ps. 30:5).

Make my mountain stand strong
by Your favor (Ps. 30:7).

Because of Your favor, the enemy will
not triumph over me (Ps. 41:11).

Through Your favor, I am brought
back from captivity (Ps. 85:1).

Let my horn be exalted through Your favor (Ps. 89:17).

My set time of favor has come (Ps. 102:13).

I entreat Your favor with my whole heart (Ps. 119:58).

Let Your favor be as a cloud of the
latter rain (Prov. 16:15).

Let Your favor be upon my life as the
dew upon the grass (Prov. 19:12).

I choose Your loving favor rather than
gold and silver (Prov. 22:1).

Let me be highly favored (Luke 1:28)

Show me Your marvelous loving-kindness (Ps. 17:7).

Remember Your mercy and loving-
kindness in my life (Ps. 25:6).

Your loving-kindness is before my eyes (Ps. 26:3).

I receive Your excellent loving-kindness (Ps. 36:7).

Continue Your loving-kindness in my life (Ps. 36:10).

Let Your loving-kindness and Your truth
continually preserve me (Ps. 40:11).

Command Your loving-kindness
in the daytime (Ps. 42:8).

Your loving-kindness is good: turn unto me according
to the multitude of Your tender mercies (Ps. 69:16).

Quicken me after Thy loving-kindness (Ps. 119:88, KJV).

Hear my voice according to Your
loving-kindness (Ps. 119:149).

You have drawn me with Your loving-
kindness (Jer. 32:18).

CHAPTER 1

BLESSING BY ASKING

ASKING FOR WHAT we need or want from God is a foundational principle of our relationship with Him as king and ruler over all. He has made Himself available to hear our request. Matthew 7:7–11 (KJV) makes that clear:

> Ask, and it shall be given you; seek, and ye shall find; knock, and it shall be opened unto you: for every one that asketh receiveth; and he that seeketh findeth; and to him that knocketh it shall be opened. Or what man is there of you, whom if his son ask bread, will he give him a stone? Or if he ask a fish, will he give him a serpent? If ye then, being evil, know how to give good gifts unto your children, how much more shall your Father

which is in heaven give good things to them
that ask him?

God's covenant leaders understood this aspect
of mankind's relationship to God, and they took
advantage of it when they came into His presence.

JABEZ—OH, THAT THOU
WOULDEST BLESS ME

The story of Jabez is only two verses (1 Chron. 4:9–10),
but it is a powerful reminder of the effectiveness of
fervent prayer. The Bible says that Jabez was an honorable man, more honorable than his brothers. Being
honorable and having a pure heart before God always
play a part in how God answers our prayers. You will
see this theme throughout this book. It's not about
being perfect, but it is about being holy, as we will
uncover later.

The story of Jabez goes on to reveal that he called
on the God of Israel, asking for a blessing, and God
granted him that which he requested. God answered
Jabez. Jabez didn't go into some long exercise of prayer,
reciting the Torah and using big words. He simply
went before God and said, "'Oh, that You would bless
me indeed, and enlarge my territory, that Your hand
would be with me, and that You would keep me from

evil, that I may not cause pain!' So God granted him what he requested" (v. 10). He asked and God gave it to him. Simple.

This teaches us that we can ask God to bless us and that He will grant us what we ask for. Jabez asked for God to bless Him, and He did. God is the source of blessing, and it is the nature of God to be good to His creation. The psalmist says, "The LORD is good, His mercy is everlasting" (Ps. 100:5). A revelation of the goodness of God will cause faith for His blessings.

JACOB—I WILL NOT LET GO UNLESS YOU BLESS ME

> Then Jacob was left alone; and a Man wrestled with him until the breaking of day. Now when He saw that He did not prevail against him, He touched the socket of his hip; and the socket of Jacob's hip was out of joint as He wrestled with him. And He said, "Let Me go, for the day breaks." But he said, "I will not let You go unless You bless me!"
>
> —Genesis 32:24–26

This event in Jacob's life came after a long battle for the woman of his dreams. He had diligently worked for his wife Rachel for a total of fourteen years. He had hope and expectation behind his efforts. Many of us pray once and immediately get angry with God when He doesn't give us what we prayed for. Not Jacob; he held on to what he knew God had for him at the end of his labor. He had his eyes set on his blessing and wouldn't let go until he had it.

But here we see Jacob once again in the midst of a battle, but this one was not a battle of flesh and blood. He is contending with the supernatural. Jacob had been taught by the fathers of past generations (Abraham and Isaac) about the power and provision of the one true God. He knew that as he came in contact with Him he had an open invitation to request a blessing. And a blessing is what he got.

> So He said to him, "What is your name?" And he said, "Jacob." And He said, "Your name shall no longer be called Jacob, but Israel; for you have struggled with God and with men, and have prevailed." Then Jacob asked, saying, "Tell me Your name, I pray." And He said, "Why is it that you ask about My name?" And He blessed him there. And Jacob called

the name of the place Peniel: "For I have seen
God face to face, and my life is preserved."
—Genesis 32:27–30

Not only did Jacob come face-to-face with God, but
because he asked, he was also blessed with a new name,
purpose, future, and destiny. His whole identity was
changed. Jacob experienced what is called a bonanza
or a "suddenly" of God. He was instantly taken from
being second after Esau, having no inheritance of
his own, to being blessed spiritually with an eternal
birthright full of the riches of the kingdom of God.

That is what God wants to do for you when you
come to Him for a blessing. He wants to give you
more than what you ask for because He is good and
because He knows how to give good gifts to His children. What you ask Him for is only the start of what
He wants to do in your life.

MOSES—PLEASE, SHOW ME YOUR GLORY

Moses longed for the glory of the Lord. He longed to
dwell in the shadow of the Almighty. He sought hard
after God, and God knew him intimately: "...for
you have found grace in My sight, and I know you
by name" (Exod. 33:17). So when the time came for
Moses to make his request to see the glory of God, he

didn't have to make a case for how close he and God were. God knew him by name. Does God know you by name?

In Exodus 33:17–23 we witness the exchange between Moses and God. The Lord granted Moses's request because Moses had found favor in His sight, and He caused His goodness to pass before Moses. Goodness is the word *tuwb*, meaning goods, good things, goodness, property, fairness, beauty, joy, and prosperity.

The Lord is abundant in goodness and is anxious to give good gifts to His children. God has laid up His goodness (blessings) for us. If we know Him and He knows us, all we have to do is ask Him for it. His blessings are for His children.

> Oh how great is thy goodness, which thou hast laid up for them that fear thee; which thou hast wrought for them that trust in thee before the sons of men!
>
> —Psalm 31:19, KJV

PRAYERS FOR BLESSING

Lord, You are the source of my blessing.

Lord, I choose blessing by walking in Your covenant.

Lord, command Your blessing upon my life.

Lord, You are the father of lights, and You give good gifts. Release Your gifts into my life (James 1:17).

Lord, I trust in You, and I receive Your blessing.

Lord, I ask and I receive Your blessing.

Lord, I seek and find Your blessing.

Lord, I knock, and the door of blessing is opened to me.

Lord, I ask for blessings in the name of Jesus, and I believe You give them to me.

Lord, You are a God who blesses and rewards those who diligently seek after You (Heb. 11).

Lord, You are a fountain of (life) blessing.

Lord, You are a tree of (life) blessing.

Lord, release Your river of blessing into my life.

Lord, rain upon my life, and pour out Your blessing over me.

Lord, release the blessing of heaven and the blessing of the deep into my life (Gen. 49:25).

Lord, release the blessing of the breast and the womb into my life (Gen. 49:25).

Let the blessing of Abraham come on my life (Gal. 3:13–14).

Let me be blessed with authority (Gen. 49:10).

Let me be a fruitful bough whose branches run over the wall (Gen. 49:22).

Lord, bless my substance and the work
of my hands (Deut. 33:11).

Lord, bless my land, and let the dew of
heaven be upon me (Deut. 33:13).

Lord, enlarge me like Gad (Deut. 33:20).

Lord, let me be satisfied with favor, and let me be
full of Your blessing like Naphtali (Deut. 33:23).

Lord, let me dwell in safety, and cover
me like Benjamin (Deut. 33:12).

Let me suck of the abundance of the seas
and of treasures hid in the sand, like
Zebulun and Issachar (Deut. 33:18–19).

Let me reap a hundredfold like Isaac (Gen. 26:12).

Let me be blessed like Jacob (Gen. 28:1).

Lord, Jabez asked You to bless him, and You
did. Bless me like Jabez (1 Chron. 4:10).

Lord, bless me and make me fruitful
like Ishmael (Gen. 17:20).

Lord, bless me with a blessing that
cannot be reversed (Num. 23:20).

Let my basket and store be blessed (Deut. 28:5).

Lord, bless my beginning and my
latter end like Job's (Job 42:12).

Lord, bless me with favor like Esther (Esther 2:17).

Lord, bless me with wisdom like Solomon.

Lord, give me favor like Nehemiah to finish the
assignment You have given me (Neh. 2:5).

Lord, bless me to inherit my territory
like Caleb and Joshua.

Lord, let me win every battle like David.

PRAYERS FOR THE BLESSING OF GOODNESS

I receive Your blessings of goodness, and You set
a crown of pure gold on my head (Ps. 21:3).

I will rejoice because of Your goodness (Exod. 18:9).

Let Your goodness pass before me (Exod. 33:19).

Let Your abundant goodness come
into my life (Exod. 34:6).

Let Your promise of goodness be
fulfilled in my life (2 Sam. 7:28).

Let me be glad and joyful because of
Your goodness (1 Kings 8:66).

I will rejoice in Your goodness (2 Chron. 6:41).

Let me delight myself in Your great
goodness (Neh. 9:25).

Let goodness and mercy follow me all the
days of my life, for You are my shepherd,
and I will not want (Ps. 23).

Remember me for Your goodness' sake (Ps. 25:7).

I will see Your goodness in the land
of the living (Ps. 27:13).

Lord, You have laid up Your great
goodness for me (Ps. 31:19).

Let Your goodness endure continually
in my life (Ps. 52:1).

Crown my year with Your goodness, and
drop fatness on my life (Ps. 65:11).

Let me be satisfied with the goodness
of Your house (Ps. 65:4).

I will praise You for Your goodness and Your
wonderful works toward me (Ps. 107:8).

Fill my soul with Your goodness (Ps. 107:9).

I receive your loving-kindness and
great goodness (Isa. 63:7).

Bring me into a plentiful country, and let
me enjoy Your goodness (Jer. 2:7).

Let me enjoy Your goodness, Lord—the
wheat, the wine, and the oil (Jer. 31:12).

Satiate my soul with fatness, and let me be
satisfied with Your goodness (Jer. 31:14).

Let men hear of the goodness and prosperity
You establish in my life (Jer. 33:9).

Let Your goodness be as the morning cloud
and as the early dew (Hosea 6:4).

Make me cheerful with Your goodness (Zech. 9:17).

I have tasted and seen that You are good (Ps. 34:8).

I will not lack any good thing (Ps. 34:10).

Do good in Your good pleasure toward me (Ps. 51:18).

Lord, withhold no good thing from me (Ps. 84:11).

Lord, give me that which is good, and
let me increase (Ps. 85:12).

Show me a token for good (Ps. 86:17).

Satisfy my mouth with good things, and let my
youth be restored as the eagle's (Ps. 103:5).

Open Your hand and fill me with good (Ps. 104:28).

Bless me out of Zion, and let me see good (Ps. 128:5).

Let me be satisfied with good by the
fruit of my mouth (Prov. 12:14).

PRAYERS FOR BONANZAS AND BREAKTHROUGH

Lord, let my desire come, and let it
be a tree of life (Prov. 13:12).

Let understanding be a wellspring
of life for me (Prov. 16:22).

Lord, let Your fear give me life (blessing); let me be
satisfied, and let me not be visited with evil (Prov. 19:23).

Lord, let humility and Your fear bring riches,
life (blessing), and honor (Prov. 22:4).

I will live and not die, and will
declare the work of the Lord.

Lord, show me the path of life; in Your
presence is fullness of joy; at Your right hand
are pleasures forevermore (Ps. 16:11).

Lord, give me life and length of days (Ps. 21:4).

Lord, give me Your favor, for in
Your favor is life (Ps. 30:5).

For with You is the fountain of life; in Your
light shall we see light (Ps. 36:9).

Let Your wisdom be a tree of life to me (Prov. 3:18).

Let Your words be life to my soul and
grace to my neck (Prov. 3:22).

I will hold fast to instruction because
it is my life (Prov. 4:13).

I have found wisdom, I have found life,
and I obtain Your favor (Prov. 8:35).

Lord, You have redeemed my life from
destruction. You crown me with loving-
kindness and tender mercies (Ps. 103:4).

Let me enjoy the blessing of fruitfulness
and multiplication (Gen. 1:22).

Let Your blessing come upon my family (Gen. 12:3).

I am blessed through Christ, the seed
of Abraham (Gen. 22:18).

Let me be blessed greatly (Gen. 24:35).

Let those connected to me be blessed (Gen. 30:27).

Let me receive blessed advice (1 Sam. 25:33).

I walk not in the counsel of the ungodly, I
stand not in the way of sinners, and I sit not
in the seat of the scornful, but I delight in the
law of the Lord, and I am blessed (Ps. 1).

Bless me, Lord, for I put my trust in You (Ps. 2:12).

Lord, I receive Your blessing for my transgression
is forgiven and my sin is covered (Ps. 32:1).

Lord, bless me; I renounce and turn away from all
guile, and iniquity is not imputed to me (Ps. 32:2).

Lord, bless me; You are my trust. I respect not the
proud nor such as turn aside to lies (Ps. 40:4).

Lord, bless me; I consider the poor. Deliver me
in the time of trouble, preserve me, and keep me
alive. Bless me upon the earth, and deliver me
not unto the will of my enemies (Ps. 41:1–2).

Lord, bless me for You have chosen me and
caused me to approach unto You and dwell
in Your courts, that I might be satisfied with
the goodness of Your house (Ps. 65:4).

Lord, daily load me with benefits (Ps. 68:19).

Lord, bless me as I dwell in Your house
and continue to praise You (Ps. 84:4).

Bless me, Lord; my strength is in You (Ps. 84:5).

Bless me, Lord, and let the light of Your countenance
shine on me; I know the joyful sound (Ps. 89:15).

Let me be blessed by Your correction, and
teach me out of Your Word (Ps. 94:12).

Bless me, Lord, and let me keep Your judgments
and do righteousness at all times (Ps. 106:3).

Bless me, Lord, for I fear You and delight
greatly in Your commandments (Ps. 112:1).

Bless me, Lord; I fear You and walk
in Your ways (Ps. 128:1).

Bless me, Lord; I receive wisdom, watching
daily at wisdom's gates, waiting at the
posts of wisdom's doors (Prov. 8:34).

Lord, I have a bountiful (generous)
eye; bless me (Prov. 22:9).

Bless me, Lord; I wait on You (Isa. 30:18).

I sow beside all waters; bless me, Lord (Isa. 32:20).

Bless me, Lord; I will not labor in vain or
bring forth for trouble (Isa. 65:23).

Bless me, Lord. I trust in You, and
my hope is in You (Jer. 17:7).

Let all nations call me blessed, and let me
be a delightful land (Mal. 3:12).

Anoint me for breakthrough (Isa. 61).

Let me experience breakthroughs
in every area of my life.

Let me break through all limitations and obstacles.

I will expand my tent, lengthen my cords,
and strengthen my stakes, because I will
experience breakthrough (Isa. 54).

The Lord my breaker goes before me (Mic. 2:13).

Let me break through in my finances.

Let me break through in relationships.

Let me break through in my health with healing.

Let me break through in my ministry.

Let me break through in my city.

Let me break through in my emotions.

Let me break through in my praise.

Let me break through in my prayer life.

Let me break through in my worship,

Let me break through in my revelation.

Let me break through in my career.

Let me break through in my giving.

Let me experience bonanzas in my life.

Let me experience Your "suddenlies," Lord.

Do a quick work in my life.

Let me experience great increase
in a short period of time.

I believe in and confess BONANZAS for my life.

Let me find the vein of prosperity
and experience bonanzas.

CHAPTER 2

THE BLESSING OF OBEDIENCE

WE KNOW FROM the story of the Fall in the Garden of Eden that our isntimacy with God rests on our obedience to Him. And if we are not close to God through obedience, we are separated from Him through our disobedience and therefore forfeit receiving His blessing.

Adam and Eve were given a simple charge, and that was to stay away from the tree of the knowledge of good and evil. Any other bountiful blessing and experience in the garden was theirs:

> And the LORD God commanded the man, saying, "Of every tree of the garden you may freely eat; but of the tree of the knowledge of

good and evil you shall not eat, for in the day
that you eat of it you shall surely die."

—Genesis 2:16–17

But they did not heed the voice of the Lord and, as
we all know, lost their place of honor, blessing, and
protection from the consequences of sin.

It is even clearer that the blessings of God depend
on our obedience when we go back and review the
Book of Deuteronomy, where God spelled out His
covenant plan to the children of Israel. It almost
seems as though He repeated Himself too much, but
we know from the Old Testament account and our
own life experience that even with His faithfulness in
reminding us of the blessing of obedience, man still
goes his own way and moves himself out of the path
of blessing.

In Deuteronomy 11, God laid out His plan for how
His children can receive His blessing. If they were
careful to do all he commanded, His blessings would
flow out to them, the children, their cattle, and their
servants. Everything their hand touched or foot tread
upon would not only be successful—but it also would
be theirs.

Imagine this kind of blessing over your business,

career, or ministry. Imagine this blessing over your home and finances, your education, and all the things that concern your family. God desires to release this kind of blessing over you, because it testifies of His goodness among the nations. When God's people prosper, not only do they look good, but God also looks good.

Reading further, you see that the children of Israel would also have the protection of the Lord from all their surrounding enemies (Deut. 11:22–25). He was declaring Himself to be their strong tower. This is what obedience will bring to you as well. Obedience brings protection from death and defeat of all kinds. In Romans 6:23, the Bible says that "the wages of sin is death." So if you obey God, you will be blessed with life. Death is a curse that Jesus died on the cross to release you from. He recaptured the blessing of an abundant life for you. All you have to do is receive His gift and walk in it by being obedient to His Word. The choice is yours.

> See, I am setting before you today a blessing and a curse—the blessing if you obey the commands of the LORD your God that I am giving you today; the curse if you disobey the commands of the LORD your God and turn

from the way that I command you today by
following other gods, which you have not
known.

—Deuteronomy 11:26–28, NIV

OBEDIENCE AS A SIGN OF TRUE FAITH

We are exercising our confession of faith and
commitment of love to God when we choose to obey
Him. (See 1 John 5:2–3.) If we only say with our
mouth that we believe in God yet do nothing of what
He tells us, we are no different from the devils and
demons who tremble and believe (James 2:17–19).
Active faith is what breeds the perfect environment
for the supernatural blessing of God. When you have
an active faith, you can receive supernatural healing,
deliverance, divine warnings of danger up ahead,
provision, and protection.

Your active faith allows you to stay connected to
and abiding in the vine. Psalm 91 is a perfect example
of one who is walking in the blessing of obedience.

Your obedience to God's direction and instruction for your life says that you trust and believe that
He knows what's best for you, that you honor your
commitment to follow Him, and that you understand
that your perspective on overcoming life's challenges

are limited. Anything less than obedience is just lip service.

In order to receive the blessing of God, you must demonstrate that He is Lord of your life. Obedience is the testing ground that proves that. He wants you to be His, and He wants to be yours. He has life for you, but you have to give your broken-down life back to Him and follow His plan for success, prosperity, and peace.

If you are a parent, you may understand it better in these terms: You tell your child to stay close to the front yard. "Stay where I can see you," you say. If your child goes outside of the boundaries you set, how can you protect them if a car comes speeding up the street or a questionable person approaches them with a piece of candy? Obedience is a lifesaver in many cases.

Obedience says, "God, I trust You with my life. Therefore I will love You by keeping Your Word in my heart so that I will not sin against You and risk losing Your favor and blessing, because they are life and breath to me."

> You shall love the LORD your God with all your heart, with all your soul, with all your strength, and with all your mind.
>
> —Luke 10:27

PRAYERS FOR THE BLESSING OF OBEDIENCE

I am willing and obedient. Let me eat
the good of the land (Isa. 1:19).

Like Christ, let me be a son who learns
obedience by the things I suffer (Heb. 5:8).

As an obedient child, I will not conform
myself to the former lusts (1 Pet. 1:14).

May I walk in Your authority so that all
the congregation of the children of God
may be obedient (Num. 27:20).

Let me not be like the nations the Lord
destroyed before me. I will be obedient to the
voice of the Lord my God (Deut. 8:20).

The rebuke of the wise is like an earring of gold and an
ornament of fine gold to my obedient ear (Prov. 25:12).

Through You I have received grace and
apostleship for obedience to the faith among
all nations for His name (Rom. 1:5).

Let me put myself to the test, whether I am
obedient in all things (2 Cor. 2:9).

I know that Your affections are greater for me
as You remember my obedience, how with fear
and trembling I received You (2 Cor. 7:15).

Lord, I pray that You will have confidence
in my obedience, knowing that I will do
even more than You say (Philem. 21).

All that the Lord has said I will do
and be obedient (Exod. 24:7).

Let me not be like those who would not walk in Your ways and weren't obedient to Your law, for like them, I will be plundered and given over to robbers (Isa. 42:24).

I present myself to obey You, Lord; therefore I am a slave of obedience leading to righteousness (Rom. 6:16).

My obedience has become known to all. Let me be wise in what is good and simple concerning evil (Rom. 16:19).

I cast down arguments and every high thing that exalts itself against the knowledge of God, bringing every thought into captivity to the obedience of Christ (2 Cor. 10:5).

Like Christ, let me humble myself and become obedient to the point of death (Phil. 2:8).

Jesus, I thank You that You made me righteous through Your obedience (Rom. 5:19).

Lord, I will obey You so that I may enter into Your rest (Heb. 3:18).

I will not obey unrighteousness. I will obey the truth. Let Your indignation and wrath be far from me (Rom. 2:8).

I will not follow my former rituals, but I will obey the Lord (2 Kings 17:40).

Let me run well, and let no one hinder me from obeying the truth (Gal. 5:7).

Because I obey Your voice, all of my seed will be blessed (Gen. 22:18).

I receive blessing because I obey the commandments of the Lord my God (Deut. 11:27).

Let me not turn my heart back to Egypt,
but let me obey (Acts 7:39).

Because I obey, You are the author of my eternal
salvation. I am perfected in You (Heb. 5:9).

I submit myself as a slave to obey You, Lord,
so that I may be righteous (Rom. 6:16).

I will obey Your voice according to what
You command me (Gen. 27:8).

Thank You, God, that as I obey Your voice,
You will be an enemy to my enemies and an
adversary to my adversaries (Exod. 23:22).

Let me not be the one who does not
obey You and receives seven times more
punishment for his sins (Lev. 26:18).

All the blessings of the Lord come upon me
and overtake me, because I obey the voice
of the Lord my God (Deut. 28:2).

I will spend my days in prosperity and my years in
pleasures, because I obey and serve You (Job 36:11).

I will obey You and incline my ear to You.
I will not be stiff-necked (Jer. 7:26).

I will eat and have enough. I will not
commit harlotry and will increase, because
I seek to obey the Lord (Hosea 4:10).

The Lord will not cast me away, because
I will obey Him (Hosea 9:17).

I will obey Your voice. I will receive correction. I will
trust in the Lord and draw near to my God (Zeph. 3:2).

I will obey God rather than men (Acts 5:29).

The Holy Spirit is given to those who
obey Him. I will obey (Acts 5:32).

I will not let sin reign in my mortal body,
nor will I obey it in its lusts (Rom. 6:12).

I will be subject to rulers and authorities, to obey them,
and will be ready for every good work (Titus 3:1).

To obey is better than sacrifice and to heed
than the fat of rams (1 Sam. 15:22).

Whether it is pleasing or displeasing, I will
obey the voice of the Lord my God that
it may be well with me (Jer. 42:6).

I thank You, Lord, that if I will obey Your
voice and keep Your covenant, I will be a
special treasure to You (Exod. 19:5).

When I am in distress, I will turn to the Lord my
God and obey His voice. He will not forsake me
or destroy me, nor will He forget the covenant
that He swore to my fathers (Deut. 4:30–31).

I will earnestly obey Your commandments
to love the Lord my God and serve You with
all my heart and soul (Deut. 11:13).

I will observe and obey all these words You
command me, that it may go well with me and
my children after me forever (Deut. 12:28).

I will walk after the Lord my God and will fear Him.
I will keep His commandments and obey His voice.
I will serve Him and hold fast to Him (Deut. 13:4).

Today I proclaim the Lord to be my God; that
I will walk in His ways and keep His statutes,
His commandments, and His judgments; and
that I will obey His voice (Deut. 26:17).

The Lord my God I will serve, and His
voice I will obey (Josh. 24:24).

I will not fear the gods of the Amorites, for You are
the Lord my God in whose land I dwell (Judg. 6:10).

Let me continue to fear, serve, and obey the
Lord, so that the political leaders who rule over
me will also follow God (1 Sam. 12:14).

Let me not be like King Saul, who transgressed against
the commandment of the Lord and feared people more
than God and obeyed their voice (1 Sam. 15:24).

Like Judah, Lord, I pray that You will give me the
singleness of heart to obey the command of my national
rulers, according to Your word (2 Chron. 30:12).

Like Esther, I pray that I will obey the commands of
the spiritual authorities in my life (Esther 2:20).

I return to You, Lord, and I know that You will
not cause Your anger to fall on me, for You are
merciful and will not remain angry forever. I
acknowledge my iniquity and my transgressions.
I have not obeyed You (Jer. 3:12–13).

I will obey Your voice and You will be my God, and
I will walk in all the ways You have commanded
me, that it may be well with me (Jer. 7:23).

I will obey and incline my ear to the Lord
my God. I will not follow the counsels and
dictates of my evil heart (Jer. 7:24).

I will amend my ways and my doings and
obey the voice of the Lord my God; then the
Lord will relent concerning the doom He
has pronounced against me (Jer. 26:13).

Even the wind and sea obey You (Matt. 8:27).

Let no one bewitch me that I should
not obey the truth (Gal. 3:1).

I will obey those by whom I am employed,
not with eyeservice as a man-pleaser, but in
sincerity of heart, fearing God (Col. 3:22).

I will be submissive and obey those who
rule over me, for they watch out for my soul
and must give an account (Heb. 13:17).

I have purified my soul in obeying the
truth through the Spirit in sincere love of
my brothers and sisters (1 Pet. 1:22).

Lord, I pray that my obedience to Your Word
will win my husband for You (1 Pet. 3:1).

Lord, I believe You and will obey You when you say to
go possess the land You have given me (Deut. 9:23).

I will obey the voice of the Lord my God, and none
of those curses will overtake me (Deut. 28:15).

I fear the Lord and obey the voice of His
servant. I walk in light and not darkness. I
trust in and rely on God (Isa. 50:10).

I receive the kingdom and dominion,
because I am a saint of the Most High. I
serve and obey Him (Dan. 7:27).

With authority I will command unclean
spirits, and they will obey me (Mark 1:27).

With even my mustard seed faith, a
mulberry tree will obey me and be uprooted
and planted in the sea (Luke 17:6).

Lord, I will obey You and will proclaim liberty
to my brother and my neighbor, because You
have proclaimed liberty to me (Jer. 34:17).

PRAYERS FOR A LIFE FLOWING WITH MILK AND HONEY

Bring me into a land flowing with
milk and honey (Exod. 3:8).

Let my teeth be white with milk (Gen. 49:12).

Let me enjoy the butter of kine and the
milk of sheep (Deut. 32:14, KJV).

Let me enjoy Your blessings like
butter and honey (Isa. 7:22).

Let milk flow into my life from the
hill of Zion (Joel 3:18).

Bring me into a land filled with wheat,
barley, vines, fig trees, and pomegranates; a
land of olive oil and honey (Deut. 8:8).

Let me ride on the high places of the earth, eat the
increase of the fields, and suck honey out of the
rock and oil out of the flinty rock (Deut. 32:13).

Feed me with the finest of the wheat, and satisfy
me with honey out of the rock (Ps. 81:16).

CHAPTER 3

THE BLESSING OF GIVING

THE BIBLE TEACHES a very simple message about being blessed to be a blessing. It is a cyclical law much like sowing and reaping. In Christian circles it has been called the law of the harvest; in the world, karma; and in science, cause and effect: "What goes around comes around." "You get what you pay for." "You get out what you put in." "Whatever you sow, you will reap." Regardless of what man has tried to label it, this law of giving and receiving originated by the hand of God at the foundation of the world. It is not a hypothesis or theory. It is an ingrained law that applies to life on this earth and in heaven regardless of if we are aware of it or not.

What you put out will be given back to you, and even more, you will receive in *proportion* to how you give. If you give (or sow) sparingly, you will receive (or reap) sparingly (2 Cor. 9:6).

If you want to receive the blessing of God, you have to be ready to give. You cannot expect to live a blessed life if all you do is receive, receive, receive. You will end up like the Dead Sea—becoming too salty and too toxic to support any kind of life. A blessed Christian is vibrant, fruitful, and able to give and sustain life. Everything around them is blessed. The spirit of death and staleness does not stay around them very long. Because they are blessed, they give blessing and in turn cause a flow of abundance in the kingdom of God where lack does not exist.

Many churches today say that they have modeled themselves after the New Testament church, but the early church received and responded to the message of giving in a way that many of us today would be reluctant to practice.

In 2 Corinthians 8:14–15, Paul encouraged the Corinthians to continue what they had always done, and that was for those with abundance to give to those who did not have so that no one would go without and that all would be blessed. He called this equality. In Acts 2:44–45 and Acts 4:32–33, it is also called having "all things in common."

There was a living flow of blessings between the members of this church. Those who were blessed gave to those who were in need of a blessing. They did this willingly and cheerfully. (See 2 Corinthians 9:7–15.) In each of these instances you will see that the supernatural grace of God surrounded and blessed the givers and receivers, so that the giving wasn't a burden and the receivers were blessed enough to become givers as well.

THE SEVEN SPIRITUAL PLACES OF ABUNDANCE

In order to receive the blessing of giving, you must first be blessed with abundance. The Old Testament names certain physical places that represented abundance, fertility, fruitfulness, excellence, and beauty. When the people of God dwelled in these places, their lives prospered like never before. They were at peace and protected from their enemies, they had all the food and produce they could eat, their land was well watered, and their cattle were fed. This was true as long as they stayed in this place.

Today, the body of Christ is struggling to understand how to be in a place of blessing and abundance so that they can give the world what it needs as a testimony of God our Father. This lack of revelation concerning His laws and ordinances about giving and receiving is what keeps the church in a position of lack. Many do not feel empowered by God's grace to give cheerfully because they are not dwelling in one of God's spiritual places of abundance.

In the Old Testament God gave made all of His blessings available to His people so that they would be a blessing to the surrounding nations and all who saw how they lived would know there was a true and living God. There were seven places where the abundance of heaven flowed down to the earth. These seven places are still active in the spiritual realm. Your prayers and confessions can begin to release this flow into your life.

Just as the Lord's Prayer says, you are able to release God's will upon the earth as it is in heaven (Luke 11:2). And it is His will to bless and prosper you.

As you learn about these seven places of spiritual abundance, begin to pray that the spirit of abundance that inhabited these places will fall on your life.

1. The plain of Sharon, the fruitfulness of the kingdom

The plain of Sharon was known for its fruitfulness and fertility. In both 1 Chronicles 27:29 and Isaiah

65:10 it was a grazing place, a pastureland for the flocks. It was full and lush, and it seemed to be ever blooming. *Barnes' Notes* on the Bible says that the Hebrew connotation of the word *blossom* in Isaiah 35:2 is that "it shall blossom abundantly... [i.e.,] blossoming it shall blossom." In other words, its fertility, fruitfulness, beauty, and life-giving ability would continue in great measure and without end. When the many-colored flowers are in bloom, it is a scene of rare beauty. What do you need to see blossom abundantly in your life? God wants to bring that beauty into your life.

2. Mount Carmel, the beauty and excellency of the kingdom

Isaiah 35:2 also mentions the excellency of Carmel, meaning that the Lord displayed His glory and splendor in this mountain. The word *Carmel* means "crimson" and also refers often to a "fruitful field." In Isaiah 10:18 and Isaiah 16:10, while the English transliteration is not used, the word *Carmel* is translated directly as a "fruitful field" and a "plentiful field" respectively. It is also referred to as:

- A place of beauty (Song of Sol. 7:5)
- Excellent (Isa. 35:2)

- A plentiful country (Jer. 2:7)
- Carmel by the sea (Jer. 46:18)

Since the *sea* often in Scripture denotes Gentiles, it is interesting to consider the imagery of the strength and beauty of the heights at the edge of the Gentiles as well as the natural imagery.

Song of Solomon 7:5 says, "Thine head upon thee is like Carmel, and the hair of thine head like purple; the king is held in the galleries" (KJV).

In every passage of Scripture that mentions *excellency* or that which is excellent, the word *Carmel* carries with it a connotation of perfection, completion, and fullness.

> But I will bring Israel back to his own pasture
> and he will graze on Carmel and Bashan;
> his appetite will be satisfied on the hills of
> Ephraim and Gilead.
>
> —Jeremiah 50:19, NIV

3. The glory of Lebanon

Fausset's Bible Dictionary describes Lebanon as a fertile valley full of fragrant flowers, aromatic shrubs and vines, cool streams, and a variety of strong and tall trees. It was a place of retreat from the heat of the plains. It was a direct contrast to the vast deserts in the area—an oasis. (See Joshua 11:17; 12:7; Psalm 72:16; 92:12; Song of Solomon 4:8, 11, 15; Isaiah 35:2; 60:13; Jeremiah 18:14.)

4. The valley of Achor

The valley of Achor is the place where the Lord's anger was turned away from Israel after Achan's stoning and they were given a pass to enter the Promised Land (Josh. 7:24–26). In Isaiah 65:10 it was a reward for the people who seek God. According to *Nelson's Illustrated Bible Dictionary*, prophets used it as a symbol of a state of contentment and peace after the coming of the Messiah—a reversal of God's wrath on men for their sins, should they receive His Son and follow His ways. The valley of Achor is like a pass-through between the curse of sin and the blessing of God, between death and life, between the old covenant and the new covenant.

5. Mount Hermon, the blessing of the kingdom, the dew of Hermon

Come with me from Lebanon, my spouse, with me from Lebanon. Look from the top of Amana, from the top of Shenir and Hermon,

> from the lions' dens, from the mountains of
> the leopards.
>
> —Song of Solomon 4:8

The dew of snow-capped, tri-peaked Mount Hermon is compared to unity—reminiscent of the Godhead. When the cool air of the snowy peaks of Mount Hermon meets the warm air of the desert, the clouds dispense a copious dew that is saturating, penetrating, and soaking. Therefore it is no wonder that at the base of Mount Hermon there are luscious gardens, fruitful orchards, and fertile fields. The dew of Hermon penetrates to the roots of trees and plants; it is not just a surface moisture.

6. Zion, the mountain of the Lord

Zion—also known as the city of David, city of peace, and city of God—was a fortress of protection for the Israelites (2 Sam. 5:7). It was the place where King David housed the ark of the covenant. It was a place of holiness, where the presence and goodness of God dwelled.

> Therefore they shall come and sing in the
> height of Zion, and shall flow together to
> the goodness of the LORD, for wheat, and for
> wine, and for oil, and for the young of the

flock and of the herd: and their soul shall be as a watered garden; and they shall not sorrow any more at all.

—Jeremiah 31:12, KJV

7. The Garden of Eden

The word *Eden* means "delight." Adam and Eve, the first man and woman, lived in the Garden of Delight. In Genesis 2 and 3 we find that Eden is a place of God's blessing and prosperity. It was plentiful with the original variety, beauty, and fruitfulness of God's creation. Every living thing can trace its beginning in the Garden of Eden. The garden also represents intimacy, a place where man was closest to God. He walked among them in the coolness of the day. There was no dividing wall of sin at the beginning. (See Genesis 3:8.)

ABUNDANCE AND PROSPERITY CONFESSIONS

I will prosper and be in health as my soul prospers.

I will not lack, for You are my shepherd, and I will not want (Ps. 23:1).

Lord, prosper me and let me have abundance.

Lord, You are El Shaddai, the God of more than enough; give me everything I need to fulfill my destiny, and let me have more than I need (Gen. 17).

Lord, You became poor that through Your poverty I might be rich.

Lord, let me not lack any good thing, for I delight myself in You.

Lord, give me the desires of my heart, for I seek You.

Lord, I put first Your kingdom and Your righteousness, and all things are added to me.

Lord, bless my coming in and my going out.

Lord, let me be blessed in the city and blessed in the field.

Lord, let me be blessed to be above and not beneath.

Lord, let me be blessed to be the head and not the tail.

Lord, let me be blessed with dominion and victory over the enemy.

Lord, let every thing my hand touches be blessed.

Lord, let Your blessing overtake my life.

Lord, let Your favor bless my life.

Lord, command Your blessing on my storehouse.

Lord, command Your blessing, even life evermore, on my life.

Lord, let me have plenty of silver.

Lord, multiply Your grace in my life, and let me abound to every good work.

Lord, let me have abundance and not scarceness.

Lord, let there be no holes in my bag.

Let the windows of heaven be opened over my life and pour me out a blessing I don't have room enough to receive. Lord, rebuke the devourer for my sake.

Lord, I seek You; cause me to prosper (2 Chron. 26:5).

Lord, speak over my life and let me prosper.

Lord, send Your angel and prosper my way (Gen. 24:40).

Lord, be with me and let me be a prosperous person (Gen. 39:2).

Let me have wisdom and prosperity (1 Kings 10:7).

Lord God of heaven, prosper me (Neh. 2:20).

Lord, take pleasure in my prosperity (Ps. 35:27).

Lord, send prosperity to my life (Ps. 118:25).

Let peace and prosperity be within my house (Ps. 122:7).

Let the gifts You have given me bring prosperity (Prov. 17:8).

Lord, You have called me; make my way prosperous (Isa. 48:15).

Lord, rule and reign over my life with prosperity (Jer. 23:5).

Lord, procure Your goodness and prosperity in my life (Jer. 33:9).

Lord, bless me, and let me not forget prosperity (Lam. 3:17).

Lord, let me prosper like Abraham (Gen. 24:35).

Lord, bless me and increase me like
Abraham my father (Isa. 51:2).

Lord, let me prosper like Joseph (Gen. 39:2).

Lord, bless me like Asher, and let me
dip my feet in oil (Deut. 33:24).

Lord, bless my house like the house
of Obed-Edom (2 Sam. 6:12).

Lord, bless me and bring me into a
wealthy place (Ps. 66:12).

Lord, give me power to get wealth (Deut. 8:18).

Lord, I am a giver; let wealth and riches
be in my house (Ps. 112:3).

Lord, Your blessing makes rich, and You add no sorrow.

Lord, bless me with enough to eat, with
plenty left (2 Chron. 31:10).

Lord, let me prosper like Daniel (Dan. 6:28).

Let ever journey I take be prosperous (Rom. 1:10).

Let every good seed I plant prosper (Zech. 8:12).

PRAYERS FOR THE BLESSING OF GIVING

It is more blessed to give than to receive (Acts 20:35).

I give, and it is given to me; pressed down, shaken
together, and running over, men give to me (Luke 6:38).

I sow bountifully, and I reap bountifully (2 Cor. 9:6).

Lord, remember all my offerings (Ps. 20).

I honor You with the firstfruits of my
increase; therefore, let my barns be
filled with plenty (Prov. 3:9–10).

I will not lack; I am a giver.

Let wealth and riches be in my house,
for I am a giver (Ps. 112:3).

I bring the tithe and offerings to the storehouse. Let the
windows of heaven be opened over my life (Mal. 3:10).

I bring the tithe and offering to the storehouse.
Rebuke the devourer for my sake (Mal. 3:11).

I sow into good ground, and I reap an
abundant harvest (Gal. 6:7).

I believe in seedtime and harvest as long
as the earth remains (Gen. 8:22).

I give, so release Your heaps into my life (2 Chron. 31:8).

I have a bountiful eye, and I give; therefore
I receive your blessing (Prov. 22:9).

I give; therefore give me richly all
things to enjoy (1 Tim. 6:17).

I will bring an offering and come
into Your courts (Ps. 96:8).

Let my prayers and giving come up as a
memorial before You (Acts 10:4).

I will support anointed ministers, and my needs are
met according to Your riches in glory (Phil. 4:18–19).

I will minister to You, Lord, with
my substance (Luke 8:2–3).

I am a doer of the Word, and I obey
Your Word by giving (Luke 6:38).

PRAYERS FOR THE BLESSING OF CARMEL AND SHARON

I receive the blessings of Carmel
and Sharon upon my life.

Let the excellency of Carmel be upon my life (Isa. 35:2).

Let my life be a fruitful field like Carmel (Isa. 35:2).

Let the beauty and fruitfulness of Carmel
be upon my life (Isa. 35:2).

Let my life be green and flourishing like
Carmel and Sharon (Isa. 35:2).

"In blossoming it shall blossom," this is Your
promise to me because of Your kingdom.

Let all my desert places bloom and come
alive like Sharon (Isa. 35:2).

Water my life, and let it blossom like Carmel.

Let waters gush forth in every wilderness
area of my life (Isa. 35:6–7).

Let my dry place become a pool (Isa. 35:6–7).

Water will gush forth in the wilderness
and streams in the desert.

The burning sand will become a pool, and the
thirsty ground bubbling springs (Isa. 35:6–7).

Let me feed upon the abundance of Carmel (Jer. 50:19).

Let Your streams flow into my life, and let it become abundant like Carmel and Sharon.

There are no waste places in my life, but my life is as abundant as Carmel.

Let joy and rejoicing increase in my life, the joy of Carmel and Sharon.

Let the majesty and glory of Lebanon be upon my life.

Let all my desert places blossom as the rose (Isa. 35:1).

I receive the abundance and prosperity of Carmel and Sharon.

Let the winter season come to an end, and let the flowers appear in my life (Song of Sol. 2:11–13).

Let my life blossom as the fig tree (Song of Sol. 2:11–13).

Let my life be fruitful like the vine (Song of Sol. 2:11–13).

Lord, let Your fragrance manifest in my life (Song of Sol. 2:11–13).

Let the blessing and prosperity of the myrtle tree be upon my life (Isa. 55:13).

Let the blessing and fragrance of the pine be upon my life (Isa. 60:13).

Let me flourish like the palm tree (Ps. 92:12).

Let me grow like the cedar in Lebanon (Ps. 92:12).

Let every area of my life grow like the lily (Hosea 14:5).

I receive the fullness of Carmel, the blessing and prosperity of the kingdom.

Let fruitfulness increase in every
area of my life like Sharon.

I receive the plenty and abundance of Carmel.

My life is changing and becoming
like Carmel and Sharon.

Let all my fields blossom and be fruitful
like Carmel and Sharon.

PRAYERS FOR THE GLORY OF LEBANON

Let the glory of Lebanon come into my life (Isa. 35:2).

Let the excellency of the cedars of Lebanon
come into my life (Song of Sol. 5:15).

I receive the majesty of Lebanon
because I am in the kingdom.

Let me grow and be strong as the
cedars of Lebanon (Ps. 92:12).

Let the beauty of Lebanon be upon my life (Isa. 60:13).

Let me ascend to the heights of Lebanon
and live in Your high places (Isa. 2:13).

Let me have the strength of the cedars of Lebanon.

Let the fruitfulness and abundance of
Lebanon be upon my life (Ps. 72:16).

Let the glory of Lebanon be released from
the building of Your temple, the church.

Lord, You created Lebanon for Your glory, and it
is a symbol of the majesty of Your kingdom. Let
the reality of Lebanon be released in my life.

Plant me as a tree of Lebanon, and let me
grow strong because of Your blessing.

Let all my waste places become like
the abundance of Lebanon.

Let the river of God flow from Your holy mountain
and water my land, and let it become like Lebanon.

Let the mountain glories of Lebanon come into my life.

Let Your rain fall upon my life, and let
me grow like the trees of Lebanon.

I will clap my hands and praise You, I will
rejoice like the trees of Lebanon.

Let even my clothes be scented like the
cedars of Lebanon (Song of Sol. 4:11).

Let the streams of Lebanon flow into
my life (Song of Sol. 4:15).

PRAYERS FOR THE BLESSING OF ACHOR

Through Christ I am redeemed from the curse,
and my Achor has turned into a blessing.

Let the blessing of Achor be upon my life.

I will lie down and rest in the valley of Achor.

I will live in the valley of blessing and
enjoy the blessings of Achor.

You have brought me to your valley of blessing, and
I will enjoy the peace and prosperity of Achor.

You are my shepherd; I shall not want (Ps. 23:1).

You make me to lie down in green pastures,
and you have restored my soul (Ps. 23:2–3).

I will enjoy the green pastures of Achor.

I will enjoy the abundance and prosperity of Achor.

Achor is my habitation, because I
am a part of Your flock.

Command Your blessings upon me in Achor.

I have left the valley of the shadow of
death, and I have come to Achor.

There is no strife in my valley, but I will
enjoy the blessings of peace in Achor.

Let the beauty of Achor and Sharon be upon my life.

I have come into Your sheepfold; feed
me in Sharon and Achor.

I will be satisfied with Your abundance
in Sharon and Achor.

I have more than enough; I live in the prosperity
and blessing of Sharon and Achor.

PRAYERS FOR THE BLESSING OF MOUNT HERMON

Let the dew of Hermon descend and
fall upon my life (Ps. 133).

I have come to the top of Amana and Senir; release the
blessing of the mountain upon my life (Song of Sol. 4:8).

PRAYERS FOR THE BLESSING OF ZION

I have come to your holy mountain, let the blessing of Zion be upon my life.

I have come to Zion, Lord; command Your blessing, even life forevermore (Ps. 133:3).

Let Your presence be upon my life continually, and let Your blessing be continual.

I receive the blessing and favor of Zion.

There is no mountain as holy as Zion; I ascend and dwell at Your holy hill.

Zion is Your habitation; I will dwell and live where You are and enjoy Your blessings.

Let everlasting joy be upon my head, for I have come to Zion (Isa. 35:10).

Let gladness and joy overtake my life; let sorrow and sadness flee away (Isa. 35:10).

Let me sing in the height of Zion, and the goodness of the Lord shall flow over me; let my soul be like a watered garden, so that I will sorrow no more (Jer. 31:12).

PRAYERS FOR THE BLESSING OF EDEN

Let all my waste places become like Eden and my desert like the garden of the Lord (Isa. 51:3).

There is no ruin in my life, but I receive and walk in the blessing of Eden.

Let me be like Eden, like a watered garden and like a spring of water, whose waters fail not (Isa. 58:11).

Let the Word sown in my life spring forth, and let me become like Eden (Isa. 61:11).

Lord, I desire that You walk with me in the cool of the day as You did with Adam and Eve in the Garden of Eden (Gen. 3:8).

CHAPTER 4

THE BLESSING OF AUTHORITY FIGURES

YOU CANNOT HAVE peace and blessing without being under authority. Isaiah 9:7 says, "Of the increase of His government and peace there will be no end." Government means authority.

Israel did not have shalom because they refused to stay in line with God's governing authority and everyone did what was right in his own eyes. But Jesus came to reverse the curse of being out of covenant and to bring peace, blessing, and an abundant life through a new covenant. He brought the authority of the kingdom, full of "righteousness and peace and joy in the Holy Spirit" (Rom. 14:17). In order to receive that, we have to be submitted to Him and to those He puts in authority over us.

When your mind is governed by the Spirit of God, when you think like a saint, when you think good thoughts, and when your mind is not controlled by your flesh and you are submitted to authority, you will receive the blessing of God. The Word of God will help you submit to His authority and not be a carnally minded Christian and expect prosperity and peace.

> For to be carnally minded is death, but to be spiritually minded is life and peace. Because the carnal mind is enmity against God; for it is not subject to the law of God, nor indeed can be.
>
> —Romans 8:6–7

As this Scripture passage says, when you are carnally minded, you are not able to be subject to law and authority. Your mind is ruled by the flesh and determined to go its own way, but at the end of that is destruction (Prov. 16:25). Some people can't prosper because of their minds. They are fleshly. But when you are spiritually minded and have submitted your thoughts to the Lord's authority, you will have life and peace, life and prosperity, life and life more abundantly.

God wants you, as a saint of God, to renew your mind (Rom. 12:1–2). He wants you to be renewed in the spirit of your mind, because "as [a man] thinketh in his heart, so is he" (Prov. 23:7, kjv).

WHO IS YOUR AUTHORITY?

Parents, pastor, professors, local and federal government officials, and boss—whether you like them or not—are whom you are subject to on the earth. You are to pray for them. You are to submit yourself to their instruction and commands as long as they do not stand in direct conflict with God's laws.

Don't think that because you don't like your pastor, boss, governor, or even the president that you don't have to respect their authority. Jesus said to give to Caesar what is Caesar's and to God what is God's. Even when you don't agree with the ruling authority in the natural realm does not mean that God has not sat that person there for a season and a reason. God establishes the authority in the earth and removes it in His time (Dan. 2:21; Prov. 21:2; 1 Chron. 29:11–12).

We may not understand why a person is in a position of authority, but God's ways are higher than ours, so as we are subject to God, we are subject to man. Even Jesus found favor in the eyes of earthly authority (Luke 2:52).

Submit to Authority and Be Blessed

So often we want to do things our own way. We even attach God's name to it, saying that we are standing up for Him. But God wants us to honor those in authority over us. Daniel is a great example of a righteous man who rose in influence in a heathen nation by being submitted to the rulers of the land yet staying obedient to God. In turn, Daniel had the king's ear for any request. He influenced the laws and codes of the day, and he was protected by angels when his enemies set a trap to take him out.

Daniel asked for special permission to not be defiled by the dietary practices of the heathen nation that held him captive. By *asking* for this, he showed submission to the authority that was over him during that time. But he was also submitted to God by his faith that if he remained obedient to God, he would be blessed in such a way that would bring him favor. And he was right. The Bible says that after Daniel interpreted a dream for King Nebuchadnezzar, the king fell prostrate before Daniel and lavished honor upon him, giving him the highest place in the kingdom (Dan. 2:46–49).

When you submit to authority, you position yourself for the blessing of God. You also are placing yourself under those who have the authority to pronounce blessing over you through prophecy, words of encouragement, promotion, and correction.

SPIRITUAL AUTHORITY CONFESSIONS

I receive the blessing of those in spiritual authority over my life.

I receive the benedictions (blessings) of my church leadership.

I receive the blessing of prophecy from those who minister by the inspiration of the Holy Spirit.

Let my spiritual leaders speak words of blessing over my life.

I receive the blessing of the Word of God ministered in my church over my life.

PRAYERS FOR THE BLESSING OF SUBMITTING TO AUTHORITY

Let me not be like the one who mocks his father and scorns obedience to his mother, for the ravens of the valley will pick out his eyes and the young eagles will eat it (Prov. 30:17).

Power and might are in Your hands, Lord. It
is at Your discretion people are made great
and given strength (1 Chron. 29:12).

Lord, You control the course of world events. You
remove kings and set up other kings. You give wisdom
to the wise and knowledge to the scholars (Dan. 2:21).

I will obey and be submissive to those
who rule over me (Heb. 13:17).

I will be subject to the governing authorities,
because they are appointed by God (Rom. 13:1).

I will pray, intercede, and give thanks for all men,
kings, and all who are in authority (1 Tim. 2:1–2).

I will remember to be subject to rulers and authorities,
to obey, to be ready for every good work (Titus 3:1).

I will not be like the dreamers who reject authority
and speak evil of dignitaries (Jude 8).

Let me not speak on my own authority but on the
authority of the Father who dwells in me (John 14:10).

I will not resist authority or the ordinance of God
and bring judgment on myself (Rom. 13:2).

Rulers are not a terror to good works but
to evil. Therefore I will not fear authority,
because I will do what is good (Rom. 13:3).

PRAYERS FOR THE BLESSING OF SUBMITTING TO THE WISDOM OF GOD

Lord, teach me wisdom's ways and lead
me in straight paths (Prov. 4:11).

The Lord's wisdom will save my life (Eccles. 7:12).

I pray for an understanding heart that is
enshrined in wisdom (Prov. 14:33).

I tune my ears to Your wisdom, Lord, and
concentrate on understanding (Prov. 2:2).

I do not put my trust in human wisdom
but in the power of God (1 Cor. 2:5).

In You, O Lord, lie the hidden treasures
of wisdom and knowledge (Col. 2:3).

I listen when those who are older speak, for
wisdom comes with age (Job 32:7).

Lord, Your wisdom is more profitable than silver,
and its wages are better than gold (Prov. 3:14).

Let wisdom multiply my days and add
years to my life (Prov. 9:11).

Let my house be built by wisdom and become
strong through good sense (Prov. 24:3).

I will not be foolish and trust my own insight, but
I will walk in wisdom and be safe (Prov. 28:26).

Let the fruit of my life prove Your
wisdom is right (Luke 7:35).

Let the fear of the Lord teach me wisdom (Prov. 15:33).

I will obey Your commands, so that I
will grow in wisdom (Ps. 111:10).

Fill me with Your Spirit, O God, and give
me great wisdom, ability, and expertise
in all kinds of crafts (Exod. 31:3).

Lord, give me wisdom and knowledge
to lead effectively (2 Chron. 1:10).

Let those who have gone before me teach
me wisdom of old (Job 8:8–10).

True wisdom and power are found
in You, God (Job 12:13).

The price of Your wisdom, O Lord, cannot be
purchased with jewels mounted in fine gold;
its price is far above rubies (Job 28:17–18).

I will keep silent, O God. Teach me wisdom (Job 33:33).

Your wisdom will save me from evil people and
from the immoral woman (Prov. 2:12, 16).

I will embrace Your wisdom, for it is happiness
and a tree of life to me (Prov. 3:18).

I will pay attention to Your wisdom, O Lord. I will
listen carefully to Your wise counsel (Prov. 5:1).

Give me understanding so that Your knowledge
and wisdom will come easily to me (Prov. 14:6).

Grant me wisdom so that I may also have good
judgment, knowledge, and discernment (Prov. 8:12).

Thank You, Lord, that You will certainly give me the
wisdom and knowledge I requested (2 Chron. 1:12).

I will not be impressed with my own wisdom, but I will instead fear the Lord and turn away from evil (Prov. 3:7).

I will not turn my back on Your wisdom, O God, for it will protect and guard me (Prov. 4:6).

Your wisdom is better than strength (Eccles. 9:16).

I thank and praise You, God of my ancestors, for You have given me wisdom and strength (Dan. 2:23).

For You will give me the right words and such wisdom that none of my opponents will be able to reply or refute me (Luke 21:15).

I need wisdom; therefore, I will ask my generous God, and He will give it to me. He will not rebuke me for asking (James 1:5).

I pray that my life pleases You, O God, that You might grant me wisdom, knowledge, and joy (Eccles. 2:26).

CHAPTER 5

THE BLESSING OF COVENANT

IN ISAIAH 54 God promised His people a covenant of peace (shalom): "For the mountains shall depart, and the hills be removed; but my kindness shall not depart from thee, neither shall the covenant of my peace be removed, saith the LORD that hath mercy on thee" (Isa. 54:10, KJV). But Israel never walked in that covenant of peace consistently because they continued to violate it. The greatest period of shalom was under King Solomon, whose name actually means peace. He was the most prosperous king of Israel. For a forty-year period Israel lived under that promise of shalom. But then Solomon married other wives and took part in idolatry, and there was a breach or a split from the covenant God had established.

Peace and shalom come from God. Only He can

give it, and He can take it away. We also have the choice to be blessed by walking in covenant with Him or to deactivate the blessings by not walking in covenant with Him.

> I form the light, and create darkness: I make peace, and create evil: I the LORD do all these things.
>
> —Isaiah 45:7, KJV

When you leave God and break His covenant, God will withdraw His shalom and allow disaster. The enemy will come into your land and destroy you. The sword will come in the land and prosperity will be destroyed. We see that this is true based on the Israelites' experiences all through the Book of Judges. But God will send warning and correction. He began to send prophets or "covenant messengers" to a covenant people to warn them of their covenant violation to give them a chance to repent before God's covenant wrath would come upon them. The prophets repeatedly said that there is no peace to the wicked.

If a prophet tells you that you will have a life of peace and you are violating God's Word—His covenant—the prophet is lying, because you will not experience shalom or peace or prosperity if you are not living in covenant with God. When someone is wicked and unrighteous, they are not at peace. Do not be fooled.

ONLY ONE WAY TO TRUE PEACE

God promised Israel that if they would keep His commandments, He would give them that shalom. But they did not listen. However, God had a plan that would not only restore Israel, if they chose, but His plan would also extend to all mankind.

In Jeremiah 31:31–34 God told the people that they would not be able to experience His peace under the old covenant because they continued to break it. He was alluding to the fact that they would only be able to experience God's true peace by way of the Messiah. The Messiah would come to make a new covenant. He came preaching the good news of the kingdom.

The only way you can experience the true shalom of God is through His Son—"the Prince of Peace" (Isa. 9:6). Jesus came preaching the "gospel of peace" (Rom. 10:15; Eph. 6:15)—or the gospel of shalom, the gospel of the kingdom. So we have to repent and receive the gospel of peace.

You are under a new covenant when you have accepted Christ's sacrifice for you and submit your life under His authority. But when you reject Christ and His sacrifice, you reject His new covenant and the very shalom you are looking for—just as the children of Israel rejected Him when He came. In Luke 19:41–42, Jesus cried over Jerusalem because He knew that if they rejected Him, they would not experience shalom but instead experience the sword. He knew that the enemy would build a trench around them and would besiege them on every side, and not one stone would be left upon another. War, famine, poverty, pestilence, and death were coming.

When you reject Jesus, you reject your only hope for peace and prosperity.

GOD ESTABLISHED A COVENANT SO THAT HE COULD BLESS YOU

You must understand how much God wants to bless His people with peace. He is the God of peace. He is Jehovah Shalom. He is the Lord our prosperity. But Israel couldn't see what was right in front of their eyes and missed it. So now this blessing belongs to the new covenant church. We inherit the promise of shalom—prosperity, favor, peace, health, and safety—because we are the ones who through the blood of Jesus enter into a new covenant with God. What Israel could not receive in the natural we receive in the spirit. It now belongs to you!

Covenant means faithfulness. Husband and wife have to be faithful to one another. Divorce comes into the picture because a covenant has been broken. Keep a covenant relationship with God. There is a huge advantage to doing this: blessing comes with covenant. God does not just bless people for any reason. Being in covenant with God is a contract or a promise of His peace, safety, favor, protection, health, and prosperity. And God does not break His promises or go back on His word (Num. 23:19; Isa. 55:11).

Covenant with God is a mutual blessing. God gets a people, and we get God (Lev. 26:12). However, when God doesn't get a people, there is no need for the covenant. We cannot be God's own if we do not walk according to His covenant. He cannot claim us and put His name on us. We can pray for peace all year long, but without Jesus, who is the Prince of Peace, shalom will never come.

> To all who are in Rome, beloved of God, called to be saints: Grace to you and peace [prosperity, shalom] from God our Father and the Lord Jesus Christ.
>
> —Romans 1:7

Notice whom the peace goes to. This peace is not to a physical people but to those "called to be saints." The saints possess the kingdom of God. Are you a saint? This goes beyond being saved. The saints are the holy ones. It doesn't mean that you are perfect or that you don't make mistakes. It means that your lifestyle is holy. You don't *live* a sinful lifestyle. In the New Testament, the saints walked in a level of holiness. They were not liars, drunkards, or whoremongers. They didn't mistreat people. If you are not a saint, you are not saved. The verse says, "Grace [*charis*, favor] and peace to those who are called to be saints." If you are a saint, prosperity belongs to you, not because of anything you did or didn't do, but because of what Jesus did for us all on Calvary. That is the blood covenant.

COVENANT CONFESSIONS

Shalom, prosperity, and peace are
mine through Jesus Christ.

I am a saint of God.

I am a child of God.

I have a covenant with God.

My covenant is a covenant of peace,
prosperity, and blessing.

I walk in covenant all the days of my life.

I enjoy shalom, prosperity, peace, and
safety all the days of my life.

I will walk in covenant.

I will be faithful to the covenant
through the blood of Jesus.

I have a covenant of shalom, peace
and prosperity, in my life.

PRAYERS FOR THE BLESSINGS OF DEUTERONOMY 28

Lord, You keep covenant and mercy with those who
love You and keep Your commandments (Exod. 20).

Lord, You bless those who obey Your
voice and keep Your covenant.

Lord, I take hold of Your covenant
through Your death and sacrifice.

I choose life (blessing) (Deut. 30:19).

Let Your blessings come upon me
and overtake me (Deut. 28:2).

Let me be blessed in the city and
blessed in the field (Deut. 28:3).

Let the fruit of my body be blessed, and let all
the fruit of my labor be blessed (Deut. 28:4).

Let my basket and store be blessed (Deut. 28:5, KJV).

Let me be blessed coming in and
blessed going out (Deut. 28:6).

Let the enemies of my soul flee before me seven ways (Deut. 28:7).

Command Your blessing upon my storehouses and all I set my hand to, and bless my land (Deut. 28:8).

Establish me as a holy person unto You, Lord (Deut. 28:9).

Let all people see that I am called by Your name (Deut. 28:10).

Make me plenteous in goods (Deut. 28:11).

Open unto me Your good treasure, and let heaven's rain fall upon my life and bless the work of my hand (Deut. 28:12).

Let me lend (give) unto many nations and not borrow (Deut. 28:12).

Make me the head and not the tail (Deut. 28:13).

Let me be above only and not beneath (Deut. 28:13).

PRAYERS FOR THE BLESSING OF HEALTH AND HEALING

Lord, bless my bread and water and take sickness away from my life (Exod. 23:25).

Lord, bless my food and protect me from illness (Exod. 23:25).

Lord, bless my eyes (vision) and ears (hearing).

Lord, let the body You have created and given me be blessed, for I am fearfully and wonderfully made (Ps. 139:14).

Lord, bless my circulatory system, my nervous system, my endocrine system, my muscular system, and my skeletal system.

Lord, let my organs be blessed, and let every part of my body function the way You intended.

Lord, let my heart beat with the rhythm of life.

Lord, You are Jehovah Shalom, my peace, my health, my prosperity (Judg. 6:24).

Lord, you are Jehovah Shammah; let Your presence give me life and health (Ezek. 48:35).

Lord, bless my blood, for the life of the flesh is in the blood.

Lord, bless me with long life and show me Your salvation (Ps. 91:16).

Lord, bless me with strength, and let me not be feeble (Ps. 105:37).

Lord, let my hands and knees be
confirmed and strong (Isa. 35:3).

I will love You, O Lord, my strength (Ps. 18:1).

Let Your strength be made perfect
in weakness (2 Cor. 12:9).

I will not confess weakness; I am strong (Joel 3:10).

Lord, lift Your countenance (face) upon me (Num. 6:26).

Lord, show me good, and lift the light of Your
countenance (face) upon me (Ps. 4:6).

Lord, bless me and make me exceedingly
glad with Your presence (Ps. 21:6).

Lord, make me full of joy in Your presence (Acts 2:28).

Lord, let Your glory be upon my
countenance (face) (2 Cor. 3:7).

Lord, in Your countenance (face) is life, and Your
favor is like a cloud of the latter rain (Prov. 16:15).

Lord, hide not Your face from me (Ps. 27:9).

Lord, make Your face to shine upon Me;
I am Your servant (Ps. 31:16).

Lord, I am blessed because my
strength is in You (Ps. 84:5).

Let my flesh be fresher than a child's, and let me
return to the days of my youth (Job 33:25).

Lord, I am blessed with Abraham because
I believe the gospel (Gal. 3:7–9).

Let not my eye become dim or my natural
vigor diminished (Deut. 34:7).

Lord, Your fear (reverence) is health to my flesh
and strength to my bones (Prov. 3:7–8).

Let your fear be health to my nerves
and sinews (Prov. 3:8, AMP).

Lord, I will keep Your word before my eyes,
and in the midst of my heart, let Your words
be health to my flesh (Prov. 4:21–22).

Lord, You are the health of my
countenance (Ps. 43:5, KJV).

Lord, let Your saving health touch my life (Ps. 67:2, KJV).

Lord, let my health spring forth speedily (Isa. 58:8).

Lord, restore health unto me and heal
me of my wounds (Jer. 30:17).

Lord, bring health and a cure to every area of my
life, and give me the abundance of peace (Jer. 33:6).

Lord, let me prosper and be in health,
even as my soul prospers (3 John 2).

Lord, You are the Sun of Righteousness; arise over
my life with healing in Your wings (Mal. 4:2).

Let my soul (mind, will, emotions) be
healed through Your mercy (Ps. 41:4).

Lord, heal every breach in my life (Ps. 60:2).

Lord, I believe all my iniquities are forgiven
and all my sicknesses are healed (Ps. 103:3).

Lord, send Your word to heal me, and deliver
me from all my destructions (Ps. 107:20).

Let my heart be whole, and bind up
all my wounds (Ps. 147:3).

CHAPTER 6

THE BLESSING OF SHALOM

As I mentioned in the introduction, activating the blessings of God has everything to do with dwelling in the peace or shalom of God, which is an all-inclusive word that encompasses prosperity, safety, health, protection, fruitfulness, and abundance. According to the Hebrew definition, we can substitute the word *prosperity* with *shalom* (peace).

Religion has conditioned us to believe that life should be full of trouble and that one day by and by we will go to heaven and then we will have peace. Peace is not only for heaven but also for the here and now on the earth. Your days should not be full of trouble. That doesn't mean trouble will not come, but you can stand up and tell trouble to go. You do not have to live a life of worry and anxiety. Peace is yours.

Prosperity is yours. Even when trouble comes, it will not take away your peace.

The whole world is looking for peace. But there is only one way to peace, and that is through Jesus. He says, "I am the way…" (John 14:6); "I am The-LORD-Is-Peace [Jehovah Shalom]" (Judg. 6:24). Having Jesus in your heart is the way of peace. No Jesus; no peace. That's when prosperity comes; that is when blessing comes. Peace is what you have as a saint of God. You are also a peacemaker, and according to Matthew 5:9, you are blessed. You bring shalom wherever you go because Jesus is inside of you. You can change the whole atmosphere of a room, because the Prince of Peace lives inside of you. This is your covenant.

> How beautiful are the feet of those who preach the gospel of peace, who bring glad tidings of good things!
>
> —Romans 10:15

The gospel is that Jesus Christ came and died so that you could experience the shalom of God. The chastisement—the price—of our peace was upon Him. He was beaten and crucified so we could have peace. All who believe and come under the rule of the Messiah can have peace.

You can have prosperity and live in safety, and all the evil beasts will be driven from your life. You will not be tormented by devils. You will have the blessing of God. It's the guarantee of His covenant of peace. It belongs to the saints of God. So no matter how bad the news gets, don't let the devil take your peace and your shalom away from you.

No matter what goes on, say, "Jehovah Shalom, You are my peace. You are my prosperity. You're the one who gives me shalom. I refuse to be tormented by the devil, to be vexed, harassed, oppressed, poor, or broke. I refuse to not have the peace of God because Jesus was chastised for my peace. I am a saint of God. I am in covenant. I have a right to peace. I can walk in that covenant. A thousand can fall at my side and ten thousand at my right hand, but it will not come nigh me, because I have a covenant of shalom."

Realize that it is not something coming one day. It's here, and it's yours. Jesus is the Prince of Peace. Do you have Jesus on the inside of you? His peace is supernatural. It's already done. All you have to do is walk in faith, and it's yours. This is why Jesus came.

KINGDOM PEACE IN A CHAOTIC WORLD

> For the kingdom of God is not eating and
> drinking, but righteousness and peace and
> joy in the Holy Spirit.
>
> —Romans 14:17

Peace is the kingdom of God. If you're not in the kingdom, you don't have shalom. If you call yourself a child of God, but you keep up a lot of confusion, there's something wrong. A child of God is a peacemaker (Rom. 12:18; Heb. 12:14). Are you a peaceable person? Do you like mess? The church is intended by God to be a model of shalom to the world.

When the world is struggling to find peace, where can they go? Whom can they turn to? Where is the model for peace? Whom can the world look at to see a model for peace? Whom can they look at as a group of people from all different backgrounds—black and white, Jew and Gentile, coming together and living in peace because of the Prince of Peace? There is only one place that this happens—the church, where the wolf lies down with the lamb (Isa. 11:6; Isa. 65:25).

This is a picture that represents the coming of the Prince of Peace into the hearts of people whereby they can love people whom they once hated. You can't be a child of God if you hate people. The church is the one place where we can show the world how to live in peace. That's our calling, and for it we will be blessed. Blessed are the *shalom* makers!

Sometimes we can get so caught up in strife that we begin to think that it's normal to have problems. But it's not. Command good days in your life to be at peace and full of blessing and prosperity. Speak blessing and prosperity over your neighbor, your troubled family member, and your coworkers.

> He who would love life and see good days, let him refrain his tongue from evil, and his lips from speaking deceit. Let him turn away from evil and do good; let him seek peace and pursue it.
>
> —1 Peter 3:10–11

Some don't think they are living unless it's hard. But that is not what Jesus died for you to have. You can have a good life, especially when you "refrain your tongue from evil." Watch your mouth. Don't gossip, argue, fight, or add to confusion. And don't keep company with people who take part in that behavior. Seek peace. Peace is prosperity. You cannot have prosperity if you don't control your tongue. A blessed person is someone who knows how to guard his tongue.

The kingdom of God is a community of peace. Saved people are peaceful people. You can disagree with somebody and still be peaceable. Contention does not belong in the house of God—or in the lives of His people. James 3:17 says, "But the wisdom that is from above is first pure, then peaceable, gentle, willing to yield ["easy to be entreated" (KJV), approachable], full of mercy and good fruits, without partiality and without hypocrisy."

When you're walking in God's wisdom, hearing from heaven and hearing the voice of God...when you're getting your wisdom from above, not earthly or fleshly wisdom...when Christ becomes your wisdom, you will go into prosperity. One of the benefits of wisdom is prosperity. Proverbs 3:16 says that riches and honor are in the hands of the wise. The wise and prosperous are peacemakers.

> Blessed (enjoying enviable happiness, spiritually prosperous—with life-joy and satisfaction in God's favor and salvation, regardless of their outward conditions) are the makers and maintainers of peace, for they shall be called the sons of God!
>
> —Matthew 5:9, AMP

Prosperous people will walk away from a fight and confusion even if they don't get their point across. They see strife as detrimental to their prosperity. They do not make room for it in their lives. "Follow peace with all men…" (Heb. 12:14, KJV).

Peace is one of the fruit of the Spirit (Gal. 5:22). As a child of God, confusion and strife vex you and don't agree with your spirit. You can't be around that. It is not *normal*. The church is to be God's community of shalom.

> If it is possible, as much as depends on you,
> live peaceably with all men.
>
> —Romans 12:18

Prosperous people are peaceful people. They are blessed. They have more than enough. They love life and see good days. They are citizen of the heavenly kingdom of God because they have been redeemed from the curses of sin and death.

PEACE CONFESSIONS

My life is good and my days are good
because I keep my tongue from evil.

I hate evil, I do good, and I seek after peace.

I commit my life to peace and prosperity.

I will live in peace, I will walk in
peace, and I will seek peace.

Jesus is my peace.

I am a peaceable person.

He is my Jehovah Shalom, my prosperity and my peace.

I will walk in peace all the days of my life.

I will see good, I will love life, and I
will have many good days.

I am blessed and prosperous, because
I am a peaceable person.

KINGDOM BLESSING CONFESSIONS

I am in the kingdom through faith in Christ,
and I receive the blessings of the kingdom.

I receive the inheritance of the kingdom.

I receive the deliverance of the kingdom (Matt. 12:28).

I receive the healing of the kingdom (Matt. 10:1).

I receive and walk in the peace of
the kingdom (Rom. 14:17).

I receive and walk in the joy of the
kingdom (Rom. 14:17).

I receive and walk in the righteousness
of the kingdom (Rom. 14:17).

I receive and walk in the power of
the kingdom (Luke 9:1).

I receive and walk in the authority
of the kingdom (Luke 9:1).

I receive understanding in the mysteries
of the kingdom (Matt. 13).

I seek first the kingdom, and everything
I need is added to me.

I reside and live in a blessed kingdom, and
I receive the blessing of the King.

I receive the favor of the King.

I receive the protection and salvation of the King.

I will serve the King all the days of my life.

I am an ambassador of the King.

I have been translated from darkness into the
kingdom of God's dear Son (Col. 1:13, KJV).

I am in the kingdom of light.

I receive the new wine and milk in
the kingdom (Joel 3:18).

I enter into the rest of the kingdom.

CONFESSIONS FOR THE BLESSINGS OF REDEMPTION

Christ is my redemption (1 Cor. 1:30).

I am the ransomed of the Lord (Isa. 35:10).

I have passed from curse to blessing because
I am ransomed (Isa. 51:10, KJV).

The Lord is my ransom (1 Tim. 2:6).

I am redeemed from the curse, and the blessing of Abraham is mine (Gal. 3:13–14).

I am redeemed from poverty, sickness, and spiritual death.

I am redeemed from destruction, and I am crowned with loving-kindness and tender mercies (Ps. 103:4).

I am redeemed from all curses of the Law.

I am redeemed from the curse of poverty.

I am redeemed from all curses of sickness and disease.

I am redeemed from all curses of insanity and madness.

I am redeemed from all curses of fear and terror.

I am redeemed from all curses of pride and rebellion.

I am redeemed from all curses of schizophrenia (double-mindedness).

I am redeemed from all curses of rejection and abuse.

I am redeemed from all curses of family destruction.

I am redeemed from all curses of witchcraft and idolatry.

I am redeemed from all curses of failure and frustration.

I am redeemed from cursing, confusion, and rebuke (Deut. 28:20).

I am redeemed from the pestilence (Deut. 28:21, KJV).

I am redeemed from consumption (Deut. 28:22).

I am redeemed from the fever (Deut. 28:22).

I am redeemed from the inflammation (Deut. 28:22).

I am redeemed from severe burning (Deut. 28:22).

I am redeemed from the sword (Deut. 28:22).

I am redeemed from scorching
and mildew (Deut. 28:22).

I am redeemed from drought (Deut. 28:23–24).

I am redeemed from being smitten
before my enemies (Deut. 28:25).

I am redeemed from vultures and jackals (Deut. 28:26).

I am redeemed from the boils, the
scab, and the itch (Deut. 28:27).

I am redeemed from madness, blindness,
and confusion of heart (Deut. 28:28).

I am redeemed from oppression and
spoiling (Deut. 28:29, kjv).

I am redeemed from having no strength (Deut. 28:32).

I am redeemed from oppression
and crushing (Deut. 28:33).

I am redeemed from being smitten (Deut. 28:35).

I am redeemed from being an astonishment,
a proverb, and a byword (Deut. 28:37).

I am redeemed from planting and
not reaping (Deut. 28:38).

I am redeemed from the worm (Deut. 28:39).

I am redeemed from miscarriage (Deut. 28:4).

I am redeemed from my seed going
into captivity (Deut. 28:41).

I am redeemed from the locust (Deut. 28:42).

I am redeemed from being low (Deut. 28:43).

I am redeemed from borrowing (Deut. 28:44).

I am redeemed from being the tail (Deut. 28:44).

I am redeemed from being pursued and
overtaken by curses (Deut. 28:45).

I am redeemed from curses that make me
a sign and a wonder (Deut. 28:46).

I am redeemed from hunger, thirst,
nakedness, and want (Deut. 28:48).

I am redeemed from the yoke of iron (Deut. 28:48).

I am redeemed from fierce enemies (Deut. 28:49–50).

I am redeemed from the devourer (Deut. 28:51).

I am redeemed from the siege (Deut. 28:52).

I am redeemed from straitness (Deut. 28:53, kjv).

I am redeemed from all plagues (Deut. 28:59).

I am redeemed from all diseases (Deut. 28:60).

I am redeemed from the evil eye (Deut. 28:56, kjv).

I am redeemed from distress (Deut. 28:55).

I am redeemed from serious sicknesses (Deut. 28:59).

I am redeemed from sicknesses that cling (Deut. 28:60).

I am redeemed from sicknesses I have
never heard of (Deut. 28:61).

I am redeemed from decrease (Deut. 28:62).

I am redeemed from being scattered (Deut. 28:64).

I am redeemed from serving other gods (Deut. 28:64).

I am redeemed from a trembling heart, failing eyes, and sorrow of mind (Deut. 28:65, KJV).

I am redeemed from fear in the day (Deut. 28:66).

I am redeemed from fear in the night (Deut. 28:66).

I am redeemed from my life hanging in doubt (Deut. 28:66).

I am redeemed from the bondage of Egypt (Deut. 28:68).

My soul is redeemed, and I will not be desolate (Ps. 25:16).

My Redeemer is mighty, and He pleads my cause (Prov. 23:11).

I will not fear because my Redeemer helps me (Isa. 41:14).

My Redeemer teaches me to profit and leads me in the way I should go (Isa. 48:17).

My Redeemer gives me everlasting kindness and mercy (Isa. 54:8).

My Redeemer has turned away my transgressions (Isa. 59:20).

The Lord has redeemed me from my troubles (Ps. 25:22).

I commit my spirit into the hands of my Redeemer (Ps. 31:5).

My Redeemer helps me (Ps. 44:26).

My Redeemer has delivered me from the power of the grave (Ps. 49:15).

I will greatly rejoice and sing, for the Lord has redeemed me (Ps. 71:23).

I am redeemed from deceit and violence (Ps. 72:14, KJV).

My Redeemer remembers me (Ps. 74:2).

I am redeemed from the hand of the enemy and from them who hate me (Ps. 107:2).

I am redeemed from all my iniquities (Ps. 130:8).

I am converted and redeemed with righteousness (Isa. 1:27).

No lions or ravenous beasts are in my path; I am redeemed (Isa. 35:9).

My transgressions have been blotted out by my Redeemer (Isa. 44:22).

Let the heavens and the earth rejoice and sing, for I have been redeemed (Isa. 44:23).

I have come to Zion with singing, and everlasting joy is upon my head, for I am redeemed (Isa. 51:11, KJV).

I have obtained joy and gladness; sorrow and mourning have left my life, for I am redeemed (Isa. 51:11, KJV).

I have been redeemed without money (Isa. 52:3).

All my waste places will sing, because I have been redeemed (Isa. 52:9).

I will drink the milk of the nations, for I have been redeemed (Isa. 60:16).

I am holy, for I have been redeemed (Isa. 62:12).

I have been delivered out of the hand of the wicked and the terrible, for I am redeemed (Jer. 15:21).

I have been redeemed and ransomed from him who was stronger than me (Jer. 31:11).

The Blessing of Shalom

The Lord has redeemed my life (Lam. 3:58).

I will continue to increase, for I
am redeemed (Zech. 10:8).

The Lord has visited and redeemed me (Luke 1:68).

I have been redeemed from iniquity
and purified (Titus 2:14, KJV).

I will sing a new song, for I am redeemed (Rev. 14:3).

I have been redeemed with an
outstretched arm (Exod. 6:6).

I have come to Zion, the holy habitation, for
I have been redeemed (Exod. 15:13).

I have been redeemed by the Lord's great
power and by His strong hand (Neh. 1:10).

I receive abundant redemption (Ps. 130:7).

I am justified freely by His grace and the
redemption that is in Christ Jesus (Rom. 3:24).

Christ Jesus is my redemption (1 Cor. 1:30).

I have redemption through His blood, the forgiveness
of sins, according to the riches of His grace (Eph. 1:7).

PRAYERS FOR THE BLESSING OF SHALOM

Let me know the way of peace (Rom. 3:17).

May the God of peace be with me (Rom. 15:33).

Let mercy, peace, and love be multiplied to me (Jude 2).

Let peace come to me, my household,
and all that I have (1 Sam. 25:6).

O Lord, lift Your countenance upon me
and give me peace (Num. 6:26).

Thank You, Lord, for giving me Your
covenant of peace (Num. 25:12).

I will depart from evil and do good; I will
seek peace and pursue it (Ps. 34:14).

You have redeemed my soul in peace from
the battle that was against me (Ps. 55:18).

Your law gives me great peace, and nothing
causes me to stumble (Ps. 119:165).

Let peace be in my walls and prosperity
within my palaces (Ps. 122:7).

Lord, You make peace in my borders and fill
me with the finest wheat (Ps. 147:14).

I am spiritually minded; therefore life
and peace are mine (Rom. 8:6).

Lord, You are not the author of confusion
but of peace (1 Cor. 14:33).

You, O Lord, are my peace and have
made me one with You (Eph. 2:14).

Let my household be counted worthy, so that
Your peace will come upon it (Matt. 10:13).

The peace You give to me is not what the world gives;
therefore my heart will not be troubled (John 14:27).

I will acquaint myself with You and be at peace,
and good will come to me (Job 22:21).

Thank You, Lord, that You give me
strength and peace (Ps. 29:11).

I pray that I will be meek and delight myself
in the abundance of peace (Ps. 37:11).

Let me be like the one who is blameless and upright,
for the future of that man is peace (Ps. 37:37).

Let my mind be stayed on You, and You will keep me
in perfect peace because I trust in You (Isa. 26:3).

Lord, You establish peace for me (Isa. 26:12).

I will dwell in a peaceful habitation, in secure
dwellings, and in quiet resting places (Isa. 32:18).

My children will be taught by the Lord, and
their peace will be great (Isa. 54:13).

Let Your peace guard my heart and mind (Phil. 4:7).

Speak peace to me, God, and let me
not turn back to folly (Ps. 85:8).

I pray that my ways will be pleasing to You,
Lord, so that You will make even my enemies
to be at peace with me (Prov. 16:7).

Your thoughts toward me are peace (Jer. 29:11).

Bring health and healing to me, O Lord, and reveal
to me the abundance of peace and truth (Jer. 33:6).

I will pursue those things that make
for peace (Rom. 14:19).

The God of peace will crush Satan
under my feet (Rom. 16:20).

You have made a covenant of peace with me, and
it is an everlasting covenant (Ezek. 37:26).

Chapter 7

The BLESSING of DECLARING "NEVER AGAIN!"

WE HAVE REACHED the final chapter of this book. You should already feel the heavens opening over you. Now, I want you to say with me, "Things will never be the same again in my life, in the name of Jesus!" The confessions that you will recite aloud in this chapter will turn your life around and help put an end to defeat and failure!

Even the Lord said never again.

> I will remember My covenant which is between Me and you and every living creature of all flesh; the waters shall never again become a flood to destroy all flesh.
>
> —Genesis 9:15

The Lord promised Noah that He would "never again" destroy the earth with a flood.

Moses told the people of Israel that they would see Pharaoh no more.

> And Moses said to the people, "Do not be afraid. Stand still, and see the salvation of the Lord, which He will accomplish for you today. For the Egyptians whom you see today, you shall see again no more forever."
>
> —Exodus 14:13

In other words, *never again* would Pharaoh oppress them. This was the word of the Lord first to Moses and then to the people.

I know that whatever God does is final. Nothing can be added to it or taken from it. "The enemy is finished, in endless ruins; the cities you uprooted are now forgotten" (Ps. 9:6, NLT). Cities were destroyed in God's judgment, never to rise again. Kings were removed from thrones, never to sit again.

Jesus told His disciples, "I will give you the keys to the kingdom of heaven, and God in heaven will allow whatever you allow on earth. But he will not allow anything that you don't allow" (Matt. 16:19, CEV; see also Matt. 18:18, CEV).

As a believer you have authority to allow or disallow. Don't allow the enemy to control your life. Take a stand against the wicked one. Use your authority in the name of Jesus. Do it by the power of the Holy Spirit. Don't give place to the devil. Rise up in faith and confess what you believe. Exercise your authority against the powers of darkness, and you will experience the blessings of God. It's time for you to declare, "Never again!"

NEVER AGAIN WILL I ALLOW SATAN TO CONTROL MY LIFE

Never again will Pharaoh (Satan) control me, because I have been delivered from his power.

Never again will I be a slave to Satan; I am now a servant of Christ.

Never again will I allow the devil to do what he desires in my life, but I resist the devil, and he flees from me (James 4:7).

Never again will I listen to or believe the lies of the devil, for he is a liar and the father of lies (John 8:44).

Never again will I listen to the voice of the wicked one.

Never again will I be vexed by unclean spirits (Luke 6:18, KJV).

Never again will I be harassed by the enemy (Matt. 9:36, AMP).

Never again will I be bound, for Christ has
made me free. I am free indeed (John 8:36).

Never again will demons operate in and control my life.

Never again will I allow the demons
of fear to control my life.

Never again will I allow the demons of
pride to puff me up (1 Cor. 4:6).

Never again will I allow the demons of
lust to operate in my members.

Never again will I allow the demons of
religion to make me act religiously.

Never again will I allow the demons of
double-mindedness to confuse me and
make me indecisive (James 1:8).

Never again will I allow the demons
of rejection to control my life.

Never again will I allow disobedience
and rebellion to control my life.

Never again will I allow curses to hinder
my life. I break every curse, for I have been
redeemed from the curse (Gal. 3:13).

Never again will I open the door for demons to come
into my life through unforgiveness (Matt. 18:35).

Never again will I open the door for demons
to enter my life through habitual sin.

Never again will I open the door for demons to
enter my life through occult involvement.

Never again will I open the door for demons to enter through rebellion and disobedience.

Never again will the demon of mind control affect my thinking, I sever all the tentacles of mind control.

Never again will serpent and scorpion spirits affect my life, for I have power to tread on serpents and scorpions.

Never again will I be tormented by the enemy.

Never again will the enemy be my master; Jesus is my Lord.

Never again will I tolerate the works of the devil in my life, for Jesus came and destroyed the works of the devil (1 John 3:8).

Never again will I allow passivity to keep me inactive.

Never again will I be beneath and not above (Deut. 28:13).

Never again will I be cursed and not walk in blessing, for the blessing of Abraham is mine (Gal. 3:13–14).

Never again will I say yes to the enemy.

Never again will I agree to the lies of the devil.

Never again will I compromise my standards and holiness; the Word of God is my standard, not the standards of the world (2 Cor. 10:2, NIV).

Never again will I act hypocritically (Mark 7:6).

Never again will I condemn the guiltless (Matt. 12:7).

Never again will I give place to the devil (Eph. 4:27).

Never again will I allow the enemy to control my will, but I submit my will to the will of God.

Never again will I allow the enemy to control my emotions, but I yield my emotions to the joy and peace of God.

Never again will I allow the enemy to control my sexual character, but I yield my body as a living sacrifice (Rom. 12:1).

Never again will I allow the enemy to control my mind, but I renew my mind with the Word of God (Rom. 12:2).

Never again will I allow the enemy to control my appetite, but I yield my appetite to the control of the Holy Spirit.

Never again will I allow the enemy to control my tongue, but I yield my tongue to the Holy Spirit.

Never again will I allow the enemy to control any part of my life, but my life is under the control of the Spirit and Word of God.

Never again will I allow the enemy to control my destiny, but God is the revealer and finisher of my destiny.

Never again will I allow the enemy to abort any plan of God for my life.

Never again will I allow people to draw me away from the love of God, but I commit myself to walking in love, for God is love (1 John 4:7–8).

Never again will I shut up my bowels of compassion (1 John 3:17, KJV).

Never again will I behave unseemly, for love does not behave unseemly (1 Cor. 13:5, KJV).

Never again will I be easily provoked, for love is not easily provoked (1 Cor. 13:5).

Never again will I seek my own, for love does not seek its own (1 Cor. 13:5).

Never again will I think evil, for love does not think evil (1 Cor. 13:5).

Never again will I lose hope, for love hopes all things (1 Cor. 13:7).

Never again will I give up, for love endures all things (1 Cor. 13:7).

Never again will I act and think like a child (1 Cor. 13:11).

Never again will I be passive with the gifts of the Spirit, but I desire spiritual gifts (1 Cor. 14:1).

Never again will I allow the accuser to accuse me, for I am washed and cleansed by the blood of the Lamb (Rev. 1:5; 7:14).

Never again will I allow sorrow and sadness to control my soul, for the Lord has taken away my sorrow and pain (Isa. 65:19).

Never again will I labor and work in vain (Isa. 65:23).

Never again will the heavens be shut over my life, but the Lord has opened the windows of heaven (Mal. 3:10).

NEVER AGAIN WILL I ALLOW SATAN TO CONTROL MY FINANCES

Never again will I allow poverty and lack to control my life, for my God supplies all my need according to His riches in glory by Christ Jesus (Phil. 4:19).

Never again will I lack, for I have plenty (Gen. 27:28).

Never again will I lack, for I will have plenty of silver (Job 22:25).

Never again will I lack; I will be plenteous in goods (Deut. 28:11).

Never again will I lack, but I will prosper through prophetic ministry (Ezra 6:14).

Never again will I sow and not reap, but I will reap where others have sown (John 4:38).

Never again will I carry a bag full of holes (Hag. 1:6).

Never will I lack glory (*kabowd*), honor, abundance, riches, splendor, glory, dignity, reputation, and reverence (Ps. 84:11).

Never again will I be poor, for the Lord became poor that I through His poverty might be rich (2 Cor. 8:9).

Never again will I live without the desires of my heart, because I will delight myself in the Lord (Ps. 37:4).

Never again will I allow covetousness to control my life, but I am a liberal giver (Prov. 11:25).

Never again will the enemy devour my finances, for the Lord has rebuked the devourer for my sake (Mal. 3:11).

Never again will I hold back from giving, for
I give, and it is given to me, good measure,
pressed down, shaken together, and running
over do men give to me (Luke 6:38).

Never again will I allow fear to stop me from giving.

Never again will I allow debt to control my life, for
I will lend unto many nations and not borrow, for
the borrower is servant to the lender (Prov. 22:7).

Never again will I allow doubt and unbelief to stop me
from believing in the promises of God (Heb. 3:19).

Never again will I think poverty and lack, for as
a man thinks in his heart, so is he (Prov. 23:7).

Never again will my basket and store be empty, for
my basket and store are blessed (Deut. 28:5, KJV).

Never again will I allow slothfulness and
laziness to dominate my life, for slothfulness
casts into a deep sleep (Prov. 19:15, KJV).

Never again will I allow Satan to steal my
finances, but I have abundant life (John 10:10).

Never again will I limit what God can do in
my finances and in my life (Ps. 78:41).

Never again will I tolerate lack, for my God
gives me abundance (Deut. 28:47).

Never again will I have just enough, for El Shaddai
gives me more than enough (Gen. 17:1–2).

Never again will I use my money for
sinful things (Ezek. 16:17).

Never again will the enemy hold back my blessings.

Never again will I doubt God's desire to
prosper me, for the Lord takes pleasure in
the prosperity of his servant (Ps. 35:27).

Never again will I be the tail and
not the head (Deut. 28:13).

Never again will I be a borrower and
not a lender (Deut. 28:12).

Never again will I be behind and
not in front (Deut. 25:18).

Never again will I believe I don't have power
to get wealth, for God gives me power to get
wealth to establish His covenant (Deut. 8:18).

Never again will I lack any good thing,
because I will seek the Lord (Ps. 34:10).

Never again will I lack prosperity, but whatever I do will
prosper, because I delight in the law of the Lord (Ps. 1).

Never again will I lack anointing
for my head (Eccles. 9:8).

Never again will I allow the circumstances to steal my
joy, for the joy of the Lord is my strength (Neh. 8:10).

Never again will I lack favor for my life, for with favor
the Lord will surround me as a shield (Ps. 5:12).

Never again will I walk in the flesh instead
of walking in the Spirit (Gal. 5:16).

Never again will I allow my flesh to do what
it wants. I am crucified with Christ.

Never again will walk in the works of the flesh, but I will manifest the fruit of the Spirit (Gal. 5:22–23).

Never again will I be weak, for I am strong (Joel 3:10).

Never again will I be oppressed, for I am far from oppression (Isa. 54:14).

Never again will I be depressed.

Never again will I vexed and tormented by demons, for I have been delivered from the power of darkness and translated in the kingdom of God's dear Son (Col. 1:13, KJV).

NEVER AGAIN WILL I ALLOW SIN TO DOMINATE MY LIFE

Never again will I love or enjoy sin.

Never again will I allow sin to reign in my body (Rom. 6:12).

Never again will I depart from holiness (Heb. 12:14).

Never again will I allow lust to dominate me (2 Pet. 1:4).

Never again will I yield my members as members of unrighteousness, but I yield my members as instruments of righteousness (Rom. 6:13).

Never again will I allow lust to war in my members, causing me to war and fight my brothers and sisters (James 4:1).

Never again will I allow fornication, uncleanness,
inordinate affection, evil concupiscence,
and covetousness, which is idolatry, to
operate in my members (Col. 3:5, KJV).

Never again will I sin against my brethren (1 Cor. 8:12).

Never again will I have respect of persons,
which is sin (James 2:9, KJV).

Never again will I develop ungodly soul ties (2 Cor. 6:14).

Never again will I allow sexual sin to reign in my life.

Never again will I allow my eyes to look at
perverse things, but I make a covenant with my
eyes not to behold any wicked thing (Job 31:1).

Never again will I allow perversion and
sexual immorality to control my life;
I flee fornication (1 Cor. 6:18).

Never again will I enjoy that which is
forbidden by the Lord (2 Cor. 6:17).

Never again will I act inappropriately
with the opposite sex.

Never again will I allow worldliness and
carnality to control my life (1 John 2:15).

Never again will I conform to the world (Rom. 12:2).

Never again will I allow anger to control my life, but I
am slow to anger and sin not (Prov. 16:32; James 1:19).

Never again will I let the sun go down
on my wrath (Eph. 4:26).

Never again will I let rage manifest in my life.

Never again will I lose control of my temper,
for he that does not rule his spirit is like a city
broken down without walls (Prov. 25:28).

Never again will I get angry at another person's success,
but I rejoice in the success of others (Rom. 12:10, 15).

Never again will I be possessive or
controlling of another person.

Never again will I allow a person to
dominate and control me.

Never again will I allow selfishness to dominate me.

Never again will I allow disobedience and rebellion
in my life, but I will be willing and obedient
and eat the good of the land (Isa. 1:19).

Never again will I allow addiction to control my
appetite, but I am temperate in all things (1 Cor. 9:25).

Never again will I allow unforgiveness and
bitterness to control my life (Eph. 4:31).

Never again will I allow discouragement and
depression to dominate my life, but I will praise Him
who is the health of my countenance (Ps. 42:5).

Never again will I walk in hate. I am
not a murderer (1 John 3:15).

Never again will I let strife come into
my relationships (Prov. 10:12).

Never again will I let anger rest in my bosom, for
anger rests in the bosom of fools (Eccles. 7:9).

Never again will I be envious, for love
does not envy (1 Cor. 13:4).

Never again will I allow jealousy and
envy to enter my heart, for envy is the
rottenness of the bones (Prov. 14:30).

Never again will I allow malice to operate in my
life, but I walk in sincerity and truth (1 Cor. 5:8).

NEVER AGAIN WILL I ALLOW MY
BODY TO BE USED BY THE ENEMY

Never again will I yield my body to fornication.
My body is the temple of the Holy Spirit.

Never again will I yield my body to gluttony and
overeating; I will not come to poverty (Prov. 23:21).

Never again will I allow harmful
substances into my body.

Never again will I yield my body to
slothfulness and laziness, for the lazy man
will be put to forced labor (Prov. 12:24).

Never again will I accept sickness and disease, because
I am healed by the stripes of Jesus (1 Pet. 2:24).

Never again will I join my body to anyone
other than my mate, for I have been saved and
delivered from sexual immorality (1 Cor. 6:16).

Never again will I submit my body to
any ungodly purpose, for my body is the
temple of the Holy Spirit (1 Cor. 3:16).

Never again will I defile my body, which is the temple of God (1 Cor. 3:17).

Never Again Will I Allow Fear to Stop Me

Never again will I be afraid, for the Lord had delivered me from all my fears (Ps. 34:4).

Never again will I be afraid of man, for the Lord is my helper (Heb. 13:6).

Never again will I be tormented by fear (1 John 4:18).

Never again will I be afraid of demons, for I tread on serpents and scorpions and over all the power of the enemy (Luke 10:19).

Never again will I not be afraid of witchcraft (Acts 13:8–11).

Never again will I be afraid to do what God tells me to do.

Never again will I be afraid of the enemy (Ps. 27:2).

Never again will I be afraid to go where the Lord sends me. Here am I; send me (Isa. 6:8).

Never again will I be afraid to prophesy, but I covet to prophesy (1 Cor. 14:39).

Never again will I be afraid to cast out demons (Mark 16:17).

Never again will I be afraid of being rejected, because I am accepted in the Beloved (Eph. 1:6).

Never again will I be afraid to witness
to the lost (Luke 19:10).

Never again will I be afraid of doing what
God tells me to do (Acts 5:29).

NEVER AGAIN WILL I ALLOW
PRIDE TO CONTROL MY LIFE

Never again will I allow pride (Leviathan)
to control my life (Job 41).

Never again will I allow my heart to
become hardened (Job 41:24).

Never again will I allow the Holy Spirit's power
to *not* flow in my life. The scales of Leviathan
have been ripped from my life (Job 41:15).

Never again will I allow stubbornness to control
my life, for stubbornness is as iniquity and idolatry,
and I am not stiff-necked (1 Sam. 15:23).

Never again will I walk in vanity and
vain glory (Gal. 5:26, kjv).

Never again will I walk in selfish ambition (James 3:14).

Never again will I speak in a boastful way (James 4:16).

Never again will I cause another
person to stumble (Mal. 2:8).

Never again will I walk in offense (Ps. 119:165, kjv).

Never again will I give myself to
drunkenness (Eph. 5:18).

NEVER AGAIN WILL I ALLOW FILTHY COMMUNICATION TO COME OUT OF MY MOUTH

Never again will I allow words of doubt and unbelief to come out of my mouth (Mark 11:23).

Never again will I allow cursing and bitterness to come out of my mouth (Rom. 3:14).

Never again will I allow profanity to come out of my mouth (Eph. 4:29).

Never again will I allow lying to come out of my mouth (Eph. 4:25).

Never again will I allow evil words to come out of my mouth (Eph. 4:31).

Never again will I allow a backbiting tongue to be a part of my life (2 Cor. 12:20).

Never again will I murmur and complain (Phil. 2:14).

Never again will I allow my tongue to be out of control, but I will bridle my tongue (James 1:26).

Never again will I allow filthy conversation to come out of my mouth (Col. 3:8).

Never again will I allow critical words to come out of my mouth.

Never again will I allow my tongue to be used for evil (Ps. 34:13).

Never again will I allow gossip in my life (Lev. 19:16).

Never again will I keep silent when I should speak (Eccles. 3:7).

Never again will I speak when I
should be silent (Eccles. 3:7).

Never again will I allow what others say
about me to control my life (Acts 19:9).

Never again will I allow spoken curses to hinder my life,
for the curse causeless shall not come (Prov. 26:2, KJV).

Never again will I be deceived by a
flattering tongue (Prov. 6:24).

Never again will I listen to the words
of the enemy (Ps. 55:3).

Never again will I walk in the counsel
of the ungodly (Ps. 1:1).

Never again will I listen to false teaching and false
doctrine, for the anointing teaches me (1 John 2:27).

Never again will I NOT listen to the
words of the wise (Prov. 22:17).

Never again will I reject correction from
those who love me (Ps. 141:5).

Never again will I listen to people who are in rebellion.

Never again will I make negative confessions, for death
and life are in the power of the tongue (Prov. 18:21).

Never again will I confess sickness and disease, because
Jesus took my sickness and infirmities (Matt. 8:17).

Never again will I confess poverty and lack; I will not
be snared by the words of my mouth (Prov. 6:2).

Never again will I confess defeat; the enemy comes
against me one way but flees seven ways (Deut. 28:25).

Never again will I confess fear, for God has not given me the spirit of fear (2 Tim. 1:7).

Never again will I confess failure, for I will meditate in the Word. I have good success (Josh. 1:8).

Never again will I allow mountains to block me, but I speak to the mountains in faith, and they are removed (Mark 11:23).

Never again will I say, "I can't," because I can do all things through Christ who strengthens me (Phil. 4:13).

Never again will I make excuses for failure (Gen. 3:12).

Never again will I be afraid to say what the Lord is saying, but I will speak what the Lord tells me to speak (Ezek. 2:7).

Never again will I be afraid to preach and walk in the revelation God gives me (1 Cor. 4:1).

Never again will I lose sight of the prophetic words spoken over my life, but I will war according to the prophecies given to me (1 Tim. 1:18).